Cooking Is Our Bag

Cover Design and Illustrations by Ann H. Low

OVERLOOK HOSPITAL AUXILIARY
SUMMIT, NEW JERSEY
1980

ISBN 0-9604560-0-7
Library of Congress Catalog Card No. 80-82863

First Printing   10,000 copies   October 1980

Profits from the sale of COOKING IS OUR BAG will be contributed to Overlook Hospital Auxiliary, Summit, New Jersey.

For additional copies use order blanks in back of book or write to:

COOKING IS OUR BAG
Overlook Hospital Auxiliary
Summit, New Jersey 07901

Checks should be made payable to Overlook Hospital Auxiliary Cookbook in the amount of $9.95 plus $1.35 postage and handling per copy. New Jersey residents add 5% sales tax.

Published in the United States of America by

OVERLOOK HOSPITAL AUXILIARY
SUMMIT, NEW JERSEY

Table of Contents

Overlook Hospital

Overlook is a voluntary, non-profit community hospital with a service area covering 14 northern New Jersey communities in Union, Morris, and Essex counties. Founded in 1906, it has grown from a modest 30-bed facility to a hospital of more than 500 acute-care beds and a teaching affiliation with Columbia University College of Physicians and Surgeons.

More than 20,000 patients receive acute hospital care at Overlook each year, with another 100,000 receiving care on an outpatient basis. In addition, about 2,000 babies are born here annually. The hospital is a participant in Columbia's neonatal network, designed to provide tertiary care for high-risk infants. The hospital has a medical staff of 450 physicians and dentists in all specialties.

A major new direction at Overlook in the 80's is in keeping people out of hospital beds as well as caring for them when they need hospital care. The Center for Community Health, to open in 1981, is an expression of that direction, with facilities for primary care, same-day surgery, pre-admission testing, and community health education programs.

As a teaching hospital, Overlook emphasizes the primary care specialties such as pediatrics, internal medicine, and family practice. It is also the only hospital in the state offering a three-year residency program in an emerging new specialty — emergency medicine. And because it is a teaching hospital, patient care is enhanced by the round-the-clock availability of a large house staff and the involvement of the physician specialists who teach them.

Overlook offers outstanding care in many areas, including monitored cardiac and intensive care, a wing for extended care, the Valerie Clinic for pediatric cancer care, a drug program, and a poison control center. The Center for Addictive Illnesses, established jointly with Morristown Memorial Hospital, provides residential and outpatient rehabilitation for patients with alcohol-related problems.

Overlook is accredited by the Joint Commission on Accreditation of Hospitals, the American Hospital Association, and the New Jersey Hospital Association.

Overlook Hospital Auxiliary

An important extension of any hospital is its Auxiliary, that group of community members who unite in an organization which pledges its support through financial endeavors, in volunteer service and in community relations. The Overlook Hospital Auxiliary has been doing just that since it was founded in 1916.

Today we number almost 1700 individuals who continue the dedication and loyalty that are the hallmark of the Overlook volunteer. We have 100 groups of members known as Twigs, assigned to one of our eight town organizations encompassing Summit, Berkeley Heights, the Chathams, New Providence, Short Hills, Springfield and Watchung Hills.

At any moment, on any floor in the hospital, we may be seen as we provide many thousands of volunteer hours each year. We sort mail, deliver flowers, run errands as messengers, make bedside bouquets, handle admissions and discharges; we push all kinds of carts, bringing services and treats to the patients; we serve as waitresses, sales personnel or cashiers in our shops. At home we spend many more hours on fund-raising, administrative chores and a multitude of activities.

Just as the collective efforts of our Auxiliary members have provided a sound base of support for Overlook Hospital, so have the collective efforts of our membership and friends brought about a unique compilation of recipes for your enjoyment, as you, too, become a member of the Overlook Hospital family of supporters.

Committee

Chairmen and Editors	Charlanne Lamberto Nancy Morrow
Art Editor	Ann Low
Secretary	Alice Stonaker
Business Manager	Jane Byrnes
Recipe Collection	Pat Guinivan Betty Kenny Betty Ziegler
Recipe Testing	Joanne Keith Ann Newell
Chapter Testing Chairmen	Maryann Belladonna Linda Bradley Fran Denecke Claire Hadden Joan Hyde Ann Jones Joan Murphy Jane Nocito Louise Noyes Eleanor Pappky June Riley Kathryn Senn Gini von Hoffmann
Publicity	Pat Guinivan
Typist	Barbara Biddison
Proofreading	Lee Moore

Our special thanks to Maryalice Marakas, Julie Planck and Jane Rech for their support of this project.

Introduction

COOKING IS OUR BAG is Overlook Hospital Auxiliary's first cookbook and we are very proud of it. It has taken nearly two years to collect, test and evaluate over 2,600 recipes and to select only the very best for inclusion in our book. The enthusiastic response from auxiliary members and friends of Overlook Hospital helped to make this book a reality.

The fifteen chapters of COOKING IS OUR BAG contain many unique recipes — from Baked Brie in our Appetizer chapter to Rabbit Stew in our Mixed Bag chapter. On each chapter divider page you will find a different bag to convey our theme throughout the book. You will also find recipes from celebrities, local restaurants, Overlook's physicians, and special diet recipes. We have included a wide variety of recipes, from easy family selections to more elaborate gourmet fare.

We have tried to include something for everyone's cooking "bag". We hope that after reading and using our book, you will make cooking "your bag", too.

Appetizers

Curried Melon Appetizer

1 T. curry powder
2 T. cider vinegar
1 T. lemon juice
½ c. heavy cream
3½ c. watermelon cubes

Remove seeds and rinds from watermelon; cut into ¾ inch chunks. In a small bowl, mix curry powder, vinegar and lemon juice. Let stand 5-10 minutes. Whip cream until very thick but not stiff. Line small strainer with cheesecloth; strain curry mixture into whipped cream. Mix gently; fold in melon cubes. Chill 15 minutes to 1 hour. Serve on lettuce leaves or with toothpicks.

Gini vonHoffmann (Mrs. Bernard)

Anchovy Dip

Yield: 4 cups

2 garlic cloves, minced
1 t. salt
1 t. dry mustard
2 t. Worcestershire
   sauce
1 tube anchovy paste
6 T. tarragon vinegar
6 T. minced chives
¾ c. minced parsley
2 c. mayonnaise
1 c. sour cream

Combine all ingredients. Chill. Serve surrounded by any combination of raw vegetables for dipping.

Elsie Roller (Mrs. Joseph)

Artichokes Parmesan

Yield: 3 cups

1 14 oz. can artichoke
   hearts drained,
   chopped
1 c. Parmesan cheese
1 c. mayonnaise
garlic powder

Combine all ingredients; blend well. Bake at 350° for 35 minutes. Serve with crackers.

Jessie Hassell (Mrs. Arthur)
Pat Pence (Mrs. John)
Margo Ward (Mrs. Richard)

Crunchy Avocado Dip

Serves 8

3 avocados, peeled, mashed
1 c. chopped toasted almonds
1 small onion, minced
1 T. lemon juice
1 T. wine vinegar
⅛ t. oregano
¼ t. salt
pepper
4 carrots, peeled, cut into sticks
1 large green pepper, sliced into strips
1 large cucumber, sliced
2 large tomatoes, cut into eighths

Combine all ingredients except crudités. Stir well and chill. Serve with vegetables.

Carolyn Walters

Three P's Cheese Ball

2 8 oz. pkgs. cream cheese, softened
1 8½ oz. can crushed pineapple, drained
¼ c. finely chopped green pepper
2 T. chopped onions
salt
1 c. coarsely chopped pecans
1 c. finely chopped pecans

Combine all ingredients except finely chopped pecans. Mix well; chill for 1 hour. Roll in finely chopped pecans. Serve with crackers.

Jane Rech (Mrs. William)

"Plains Special" Cheese Ring

1 lb. grated sharp
  cheese
1 c. finely chopped nuts
1 c. mayonnaise
1 small onion, finely
  grated
black pepper
dash cayenne
strawberry preserves
  (optional)

Combine all ingredients except preserves; season to taste with pepper. Mix
well; place in a 5 or 6 cup lightly greased
ring mold. Refrigerate until firm for several hours or overnight. To serve, unmold. If desired, fill center with strawberry preserves, or serve plain with
crackers.

Rosalynn Carter

Baked Brie
Serves 8

½ c. butter, melted
½ c. slivered,
  unblanched almonds
2 4 oz. rounds of Brie
French bread

Saute almonds lightly in butter. Place
each whole Brie on its own oven-proof
plate; pour half the butter-almond mixture
over each. Bake at 375° for 10-15 minutes until cheese is soft. Serve hot with
thinly sliced French bread.

Summit, New Providence, Berkeley
Heights Welcome Wagon

Hungarian Cheese Spread
Serves 25

2 8 oz. pkgs. cream
  cheese
½ lb. butter, softened
½ c. sour cream
2½ t. paprika
1½ T. minced capers
4 anchovy fillets,
  chopped
1 garlic clove, mashed
4 T. chopped chives
1½ T. caraway seeds
¾ t. dry mustard
1 t. salt
½ t. pepper
chopped parsley

Mix cheese with butter until smooth;
blend in all other ingredients except parsley. Garnish with parsley and a dash of
paprika. Serve with party rye bread.

Linda Gamborg (Mrs. Richard)

Aunt Addie's Cheese Biscuits

Yield: 24 biscuits

1 c. grated sharp
  Cheddar cheese
¼ lb. butter, softened
1 c. sifted flour
¼ t. salt
¼ t. cayenne pepper
¼ t. paprika
1 c. Rice Krispies

Combine all ingredients thoroughly. Roll into little balls the size of a cherry; flatten with a fork. Arrange on ungreased cookie sheet; bake at 350° for 10-12 minutes until golden.

Mabel Ehlert (Mrs. William)
Ruth Layng (Mrs. E.T.)

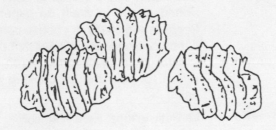

Miniature Cheese Tarts

Yield: 24

1 uncooked pie crust
5 slices crisp-cooked
  bacon
3 eggs
¼ c. sour cream
¼ lb. Swiss cheese,
  finely grated
½ t. grated onion
¼ t. poppy seeds
⅛ t. pepper

Shape crust into rectangle; cut in 2 inch squares. Press each square into a 1 inch muffin cup; put a small piece of bacon in each cup. Beat eggs with sour cream. Stir in all other ingredients; pour into muffin cups. Refrigerate or freeze. To serve, bring to room temperature; bake at 425° for 5 minutes and at 325° for 12 more minutes until brown.

Dotty Stevens (Mrs. Roger)

Cheese Toast

Yield: 4 dozen strips

1 lb. loaf firm white
  bread, crusts removed
3 T. butter, melted
3 T. flour
½ lb. Swiss cheese,
  grated
4 egg yolks
4 egg whites, whipped
oil heated for deep frying

Cut each bread slice into 3 strips; set aside. Combine butter and flour; add cheese. Heat until thick and smooth. Cool. Beat in egg yolks, spread mixture on both sides of bread strips. Dip strips in egg whites; fry until crisp and golden. Serve hot on toothpicks.

Jean Clutsam (Mrs. Henry O., Jr.)

Cheese Fingers

white bread, sliced,
crusts removed
Dijon mustard
gruyere cheese
oil

Roll bread flat with rolling pin. Brush with mustard, covering completely. Measure a piece of cheese so that when bread is rolled, the cheese is encased in bread. Roll-up bread; press ends and edge firmly. Refrigerate in airtight bag until ready to use. Heat 2 inches of oil to 400°; slide cheese fingers into oil individually. Cook until lightly browned; remove with slotted spoon to drain on paper towel. Serve immediately. If cheese comes out during cooking, edges were not properly sealed. If bread absorbs oil, oil did not return to 400° before cooking second batch.

Le Petit Village, East Windsor

Mexican Quiche

Serves 10-12

2 cans chopped green
   chili peppers
10 oz. extra sharp
   cheddar cheese,
   grated
2 eggs
3 T. milk

Spread chili peppers in buttered 10″ pie pan. Cover with grated cheese. Combine eggs and milk; pour over cheese. Bake at 325° for 30-45 minutes. Serve with fritos.

Jean Clutsam (Mrs. Henry O., Jr.)
Virginia Kent (Mrs. Donald)
Doll Siegel (Mrs. M. Alden)
Bobbie Tooher (Mrs. James)

Tangy Beef

Yield: 2 cups

½ c. sour cream
1 8 oz. pkg. cream
   cheese
2 T. milk
2 T. chopped green
   pepper
2 T. minced onion
¼ c. chopped walnuts
2½ oz. snipped dried
   beef
⅛ t. pepper

Combine all ingredients; blend well. Spoon into an 8″ pie plate. Bake at 350° for 15 minutes. Serve hot with crackers.

Fraser Grimes (Mrs. Michael)
Charlotte Nelson (Mrs. John)
Lynn Tully (Mrs. Paul)

Chicken Walnut Spread

Yield: 2 cups

1 c. minced chicken
¾ c. finely chopped
  walnuts
2 T. finely chopped
  shallots
¼ t. salt
½ t. paprika
2 T. mayonnaise
2-4 T. sour cream

Combine all ingredients and chill well. Serve with crackers or as stuffing for celery.

Frances Greenidge (Mrs. Ralph)

Satay Peanut Dip

½-1t. red pepper flakes
2 T. finely chopped
  onion
1 garlic clove, minced
1 T. corn oil
3 T. peanut butter
½ t. turmeric
½ t. brown sugar
¾ c. water
½ T. lime juice
½ T. dark soy sauce
½ t. grated fresh ginger

Grind pepper flakes to a powder in blender. Add remaining ingredients; blend until thoroughly mixed. Serve with crudites.

Kenneth D. Meals

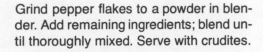

Simply Delicious

Yield: 1½ cups

3 scallions with greens
1 cucumber, unpeeled
8 oz. cream cheese

Mince scallions and cucumber in food processor; blend in cream cheese. Serve with crackers.

Marj Miller (Mrs. William)

Chicken Liver Paté

1 small onion
10-12 raw chicken livers
salt and pepper
1 t. Worcestershire
   sauce
3 egg yolks
⅔ c. heavy cream

Separate chicken livers; remove membrane. Combine onion, chicken livers, salt, pepper and Worcestershire sauce in blender until smooth. Mix egg yolks with heavy cream; add to liver mixture. Pour mixture into greased 2½ cup oven-proof mold. Place mold in a shallow pan of water; bake at 400° for 50-60 minutes until dark brown. Cool thoroughly before unmolding. Refrigerate at least four hours or overnight before serving. Serve with toast points or crackers.

John Krikorian, M.D.

Paté Bremerhaven

Yield: 1½ lbs.

1 lb. liverwurst,
   softened
4 oz. cream cheese
½ c. butter
½ T. curry powder
2 T. chopped onion
2 T. chopped parsley
2 T. brandy

Blend liverwurst, cheese and butter until smooth. Add remaining ingredients; beat until soft and fluffy. Refrigerate or freeze for later use.

Betty Gorman (Mrs. Paul)

Cheesy Mushroom Bake

Yield: 3 cups

1 8 oz. pkg. cream
   cheese, softened
1 c. grated Swiss
   cheese
¼ c. chopped onion
6 slices bacon, cooked,
   crumbled
¼ c. mushrooms,
   sauteed
½ c. milk

Blend together all ingredients. Pour into a 1 pint baking dish which can be used for serving. Bake at 400° for 15 minutes.

Joy Noel (Mrs. William)

Mushrooms au Gratin

Serves 6-8

2 lbs. fresh mushroom
  caps
1 c. shredded Swiss
  cheese
1 hard cooked egg,
  finely chopped
3 T. Italian bread crumbs
½ garlic clove, mashed
2 T. soft butter

Stuff mushrooms with a mixture of all other ingredients. Bake at 375° for 15 minutes.

Anne Callahan (Mrs. P. George)

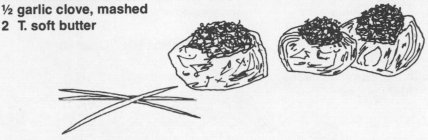

Sausage-Mushroom Bites

Serves 12

2 lbs. Italian sweet
  sausage, cut in 1"
  lengths
1 lb. long-stemmed
  mushrooms
2 c. spaghetti sauce

Fit a sausage piece onto each mushroom stem, pushing all the way to the cap. Simmer sausage-mushroom pieces in sauce for 20 minutes until sausage is fully cooked. Serve hot with toothpicks.

Ellen Eiermann (Mrs. Harry J., III)

Caviar Pie

Serves 8

6 hard cooked eggs,
  chopped
3 T. mayonnaise
1 onion, chopped
4 oz. cream cheese
⅔ c. sour cream
3-4 oz. lumpfish caviar
minced parsley
lemon slices

Combine eggs with mayonnaise; spread in buttered 9" glass pie pan. Top with chopped onion. Mix cream cheese with sour cream until smooth. Spread on top of onion layer. Chill at least 3 hours or overnight. Spread caviar on pie, leaving a half inch border. Sprinkle border with parsley. Cut into small wedges. Garnish with lemon slices.

Sally Duffy (Mrs. John)

Clams Mozzarella

Serves 6-8

1 small onion, minced
¼ lb. butter, melted
2 6½ oz. cans minced
    clams with liquid
1 t. garlic powder
½ t. Tabasco
⅛ t. pepper
2 T. lemon juice
1 c. Italian bread
    crumbs
oregano
½ lb. mozzarella cheese,
    thinly sliced

Saute onion in butter; remove from heat and mix with all other ingredients except cheese. In a shallow baking dish, layer cheese and clam mixture alternately, ending with cheese on top. Bake at 350° for 20 minutes, until top layer is melted. Serve hot with crackers. (Freezes well uncooked.)

Shirley Messina (Mrs. Charles)

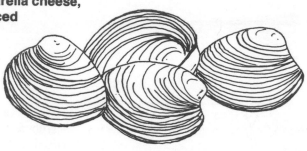

Stuffed Clams with Bacon

Serves 6-8

15 large raw quahogs or
     6-8 raw chowder
     clams
2 c. seasoned bread
    crumbs
½ large onion, finely
    chopped
2 t. chopped parsley
½ c. chopped fresh
    tomatoes
1 stalk celery, minced
3 small sweet gherkins,
    minced
1 t. Worcestershire
    sauce
2 T. mayonnaise
dash Tabasco
salt and pepper
4 slices raw bacon,
    chopped

Open and chop clams, combining with any clam liquid; reserve shells.* Scrub shells thoroughly; set aside. Combine clams with all other ingredients except bacon; stuff mixture into shells. Adjust consistency of mixture if needed, by adding extra crumbs or juice. Sprinkle bacon on top; bake at 375° for 15-20 minutes, or broil, until bacon is cooked and clams are heated through. Serve hot. (Uncooked stuffed clams can be frozen until ready to bake or broil.)

*To prepare shells: Remove muscles left in open shell; scrub exterior. Boil in combination of vinegar and water to cover for 5-10 minutes.

Karen Cooper (Mrs. Charles)

Cheese and Clam Fondue

¼ lb. butter
1 lb. Velveeta cheese,
   cubed
1 small onion, chopped,
   sauteed
1 10½ oz. can minced
   clams, drained
3 T. ketchup
2 t. Worcestershire
   sauce
¼ t. Tabasco
3 T. dry sherry
bread cubes

In top of double boiler, melt butter. Add remaining ingredients, except bread. Cook, stirring, until cheese is melted. Transfer to fondue pot; serve with bread cubes. Can be reheated or frozen.

Joseph I. Boylan, Jr., M.D.

Curried Crab Canapes

Yield: 20 canapes

10 slices white bread,
   cut into 20 rounds
1½ c. mayonnaise
1½ t. curry powder
1½ c. crab meat
1 c. shredded Cheddar
   cheese

Toast rounds on one side only; spread untoasted sides with a mixture of the mayonnaise and curry. Place 1 tablespoon crabmeat on each and sprinkle with cheese. Toast under broiler.

Isobel Mitchell (Mrs. James)

Shrimp with Brandied Cocktail Sauce

1 egg yolk, hard-cooked
1 t. Dijon mustard
3 T. olive oil, divided
1 T. lemon juice
6 T. chili sauce
2-3 drops
   Worcestershire
   sauce
1 T. brandy
2 T. cream
½ t. salt
pepper
1 lb. cooked shrimp

Mash egg yolk with mustard; add 2 tablespoons of the oil, drop by drop, stirring constantly. Gradually add lemon juice and remaining oil. Stir in chili sauce, Worcestershire sauce, brandy, cream, salt and pepper. Mix with shrimp; chill.

Joan Mattson (Mrs. Charles)

Shrimp Canapes Savoy

Serves 12

1 lb. loaf sliced white
  bread
2 4½ oz. cans small
  shrimp, drained,
  chopped
4 hard-cooked eggs,
  finely chopped
4 stalks celery, minced
4 green onions, minced
mayonnaise
1 t. lemon juice
salt and pepper

Cut each bread slice into 2 rounds; set aside. Combine all ingredients, using enough mayonnaise for a spreading consistency. Spread mixture on rounds and serve.

Deane Geider (Mrs. George)

Cheese Shrimp Strudel

Yield: 28 slices

1 10 oz. pkg. frozen
  patty shells
2 T. melted butter
6 oz. Swiss cheese,
  shredded
½ c. sour cream
1 egg, well beaten
¼ c. chopped scallions
1 c. cooked or canned
  shrimp, chopped

Thaw patty shells in refrigerator overnight in package. Place 3 shells side by side on floured surface. Place 2 shells side by side on top in center. Cut remaining shell and position on either side of top. Roll out into 8x14″ rectangle. Brush with butter. Mix cheese, sour cream, half of the egg, scallion and shrimp. Place on long side of pastry. Roll up, enclosing filling; seal ends. Brush with remaining egg. Bake, seam side down on greased cookie sheet, at 400° for 35-40 minutes. Cool; cut into 28 half inch slices.

William Kellogg, M.D.

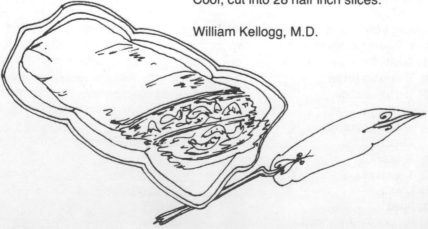

Cheddar Shrimp Canape

Serves 10-12

½ lb. Cheddar cheese,
  finely grated
1 5 oz. can small
  shrimp, mashed
1 c. mayonnaise
1 small onion, finely
  chopped
1 t. Worcestershire
  sauce
½ t. garlic salt or powder
¼ t. lemon juice
1 lb. loaf party rye bread
paprika

Combine all ingredients except bread and paprika. Spread mixture on bread slices; sprinkle with paprika. Broil for 2 minutes until golden and bubbly.

Joanne Keith (Mrs. James)

Shrimp Toast

Serves 4-6

¾ lb. raw fresh shrimp,
  shelled, minced
6 water chestnuts, finely
  chopped
1 T. dry sherry
1 egg, beaten
2 T. cornstarch
1 t. salt
6 slices firm white
  bread, crusts removed
chopped parsley
oil

Mix shrimp with water chestnuts, sherry, egg, cornstarch and salt. Cut bread in quarters; spread each piece with shrimp mixture; garnish with parsley. Drop bread, shrimp-side down in oil; deep-fry until bread and topping are golden brown. Drain and serve. May be prepared ahead and frozen; bake at 350° for 10 minutes to re-heat.

Sally Shabaker (Mrs. Robert)

Copenhagens

Yield: 4 dozen

¼ c. mayonnaise
1 T. chopped parsley
½ t. lemon juice
1 8 oz. can water
  chestnuts, drained,
  sliced
1 3 oz. can small
  shrimp, drained

Combine mayonnaise, parsley and lemon juice. Blend well and spread on water chestnut slices. Top each with a shrimp.

Nancy Morrow (Mrs. David)

Saganaki

4 T. olive oil, heated
1 lb. large raw shrimp,
   peeled, deveined
¼ lb. small whole fresh
   mushrooms
1 14 oz. can artichoke
   hearts, drained,
   halved
½ t. garlic powder
½ t. salt
pepper
½ t. oregano
2 T. lemon juice
2 T. dried parsley

Combine oil, shrimp and mushrooms; cook and stir until shrimp turns pink. Add artichokes, garlic, salt, pepper and oregano; cook until hot. Stir in lemon juice; transfer to a chafing dish or a warmer. Sprinkle with parsley. (May be prepared ahead and reheated.)

Pat Guinivan (Mrs. Thomas)

Snails in Mushroom Caps

Serves 6

3 T. minced parsley
3 T. minced scallions
3 garlic cloves, pressed
6 T. butter
salt and pepper
nutmeg
2 dozen fresh
   mushrooms
2 dozen snails, rinsed

Mix parsley, scallions, garlic and butter. Add salt, pepper and nutmeg to taste. Remove stems from mushrooms; put some of the butter mixture in each mushroom. Place a snail in each; top with more of the butter mixture. Place in escargot pans or cookie sheet. Bake at 400° for 10 minutes.

Calvin D. Low

Chicken Wings Provencale   Yield: 2½ dozen wings

5 lbs. chicken wings,
   tips removed
2 c. milk
flour
salt and pepper
olive oil
6 garlic cloves, crushed
1 lemon, thinly sliced
¾ c. chopped parsley

Soak chicken in milk for 1-2 hours; drain and dry. Dredge in seasoned flour; saute in oil until crisp and golden. Arrange in a large foil-lined baking dish; scatter garlic and lemon over all; sprinkle with parsley. Bake at 250° for 10-15 minutes.

Howard Baldwin

Almond Chicken Chunks

Yield: 50 chunks

7 chicken breast halves
1 unpeeled onion,
  quartered
3 sprigs parsley
5 peppercorns
1 t. ground thyme
1 bay leaf
1½ T. salt
1 c. white wine
  (optional)
2 c. Mustard
  Mayonnaise Sauce
½ c. unblanched
  almonds, toasted,
  finely chopped

Cover chicken with water; add next 6 ingredients and wine, if desired. Bring to a boil; simmer until tender; let cool. Remove meat from bones, keeping breast meat as whole as possible. Cut each breast into 7-8 wedge-shaped chunks. Dip wide end of chunks into sauce, then into nuts. Cover and chill 30-45 minutes before serving. May be started 2 days ahead; postpone dipping until 1 hour before serving.

Sauce: Combine all ingredients; refrigerate 2 hours or more.

Norma Horton (Mrs. John)

Sauce:
2 c. mayonnaise
4 oz. Dijon mustard
2 shallots, finely
  chopped
1 T. white wine vinegar
¾ t. ground pepper

Chicken Puffs Amandine

Yield: 2 dozen

½ c. chicken broth
¼ c. butter
⅛ t. salt
2 c. sifted flour
2 eggs
1 4¾ oz. can chicken
  spread
¾ c. diced toasted
  almonds
¼ t. almond extract

Bring broth, butter and salt to a boil; reduce heat; add flour all at once. Stir well until mixture leaves sides of pan; remove from heat. Beat, adding one egg at a time, until mixture is smooth and shiny. Stir in remaining ingredients. Drop by scant teaspoonfuls onto greased cookie sheet. Bake at 450° for 10-12 minutes until golden brown. Serve warm. (Can be made ahead, frozen and re-heated.)

Joanne Keith (Mrs. James)

Raisin Cactus

Serves 8-10

2 14 oz. cans artichoke
   hearts drained, halved
1 8 oz. pkg. cream
   cheese
⅓ c. raisins
dash cayenne pepper
½ c. Parmesan cheese

Pat artichokes dry. Combine cream cheese, raisins and cayenne; form into balls, placing one on each artichoke piece. Roll pieces in grated Parmesan cheese; coat well. Bake on lightly greased cookie sheet at 400° for 12 minutes.

Bobbie Tooher (Mrs. James)

Carrot Balls

Serves 6

2 medium carrots,
   shredded
8 oz. cream cheese,
   softened
½ c. finely chopped
   walnuts
fresh parsley, finely
   chopped

Mash the carrots into the cream cheese. Roll into 1 inch balls. Mix parsley and nuts in a flat dish. Roll balls in parsley-nut mixture.

Pag Habig (Mrs. F.)

Spinach Brownies

Yield: 1½ dozen

1 c. flour
1 t. salt
1 t. baking soda
2 eggs, beaten
1 c. milk
¼ lb. butter, melted
½ onion, chopped
1 lb. sharp Cheddar
   cheese, shredded
1 10 oz. pkg. frozen
   chopped spinach,
   thawed, drained

Combine flour, salt and baking soda. Mix in all other ingredients. Place in a 9x9" baking dish. Bake at 350° for 30-35 minutes. Cut in 2 inch squares. May be frozen; reheat to serve.

Anne Finn (Mrs. George)

Spanakopetes — Spinach Cheese Puffs

Yield: 40-50 puffs

1 onion, finely chopped
¼ c. olive oil
1 10 oz. pkg. frozen chopped spinach, thawed, drained
½ lb. feta cheese, crumbled
6 oz. pot cheese
3 eggs, beaten
¼ c. bread crumbs
½ lb. phyllo leaves
½ c. butter, melted

Saute onion in oil for 5 minutes; add spinach; simmer until most moisture evaporates. Combine the two cheeses and the eggs; mix well. Stir in spinach and bread crumbs. Set aside. Cut phyllo leaves into thirds, cutting parallel to the short side. Refrigerate ⅔ of leaves until needed; cover remainder with a damp towel. Butter one phyllo leaf; fold long sides in towards the middle, making a 2 inch wide strip; butter again. Put 1 tablespoon of spinach mixture in bottom right corner of strip; fold over to form a triangle. Continue folding so that bottom edge of each fold is parallel with alternate side edge; lightly butter finished triangle. Repeat until all phyllo leaves and spinach mixture are used. Bake at 425° for 20 minutes until golden brown, turning once. Cool 5 minutes; serve warm. To freeze ahead, store uncooked puffs in a container with wax paper between layers. Do not thaw before baking.

Tiffany Corbett (Mrs. James)

Tomato Toasties

Yield: 2 dozen

French bread, sliced ¼" thick
¼ c. chopped green onions
¼ c. chopped green peppers
½ c. mayonnaise
¼ t. salt
chopped tomatoes
bacon, cut into 1½" pieces

Combine onions, peppers, mayonnaise and salt. Spread on French bread. Add tomato and bacon pieces. Place under broiler for 5 minutes until bacon browns.

Pauline Quinlan (Mrs. Paul)

Manhattan Cocktail Meatballs

1½ lbs. ground beef
1 egg, beaten
1 t. salt
olive oil
1 small onion, minced
1 garlic clove
¼ t. salt
¼ t. oregano
1 T. flour
1 beef bouillon cube
1 c. water
1 t. dry mustard
dash Angostura bitters
¼ c. whiskey
2 T. sweet Vermouth
French bread cut in
    small chunks

Combine beef, egg and salt; form into tiny balls. Brown in oil; remove. Saute onion and garlic in oil; add remaining ingredients, blending flour and water. Add meatballs and simmer for 30 minutes. Serve plain or with bread chunks to dip in sauce.

Eileen Sheeran (Mrs. Stanley)

Zucchini Tidbits   Yield: 4 dozen

3 zucchini, sliced
3 onions, coarsely
    chopped
oil or butter
3 eggs, beaten
¾ lb. Muenster cheese,
    grated

Saute zucchini and onions in oil for 20 minutes; drain. Stir in eggs mixed with cheese. Pour into a 13x9″ baking dish; bake at 350° for 30 minutes. Cut into bite-sized pieces; serve hot. Freezes well.

Norma Lehrman (Mrs. Maurice)

Zucchini Rounds   Yield: 12 rounds

⅓ c. packaged biscuit
    mix
¼ c. grated Parmesan
    cheese
salt and pepper
2 eggs, slightly beaten
2 c. shredded, unpared
    zucchini
2 T. butter

Combine biscuit mix, cheese, salt and pepper. Stir in eggs just until mixture is moistened; fold in zucchini. For each round, drop 2 tablespoons mixture in butter. Cook 2-3 minutes on each side until brown.

Phyllis Western (Mrs. Vernon)

Pissaladiere

1 sweet red or green
  pepper, thinly sliced
2 Spanish onions, thinly
  sliced
1 garlic clove, crushed
3 T. olive oil
¼ t. rosemary
1 12″ pizza crust,
  uncooked
½ c. Parmesan cheese
4 oz. mozzarella cheese,
  shredded
1 15½ oz. jar meatless
  spaghetti sauce
2 2 oz. cans flat
  anchovy fillets, rinsed
pitted ripe olives, halved
  lengthwise

Saute pepper, onions and garlic in oil until soft; add rosemary. Bake crust at 425° for 10 minutes until lightly browned. Sprinkle with Parmesan cheese; spoon on pepper-onion mixture. Cover with mozzarella cheese; pour sauce over all. Garnish with anchovies criss-crossed in center with olives in between. Bake uncovered for 10 more minutes, until bubbly. Let stand 5 minutes, then cut.

Leanne Conte (Mrs. Frank)

Poor Man's Caviar

1 small eggplant, baked,
  skinned and mashed
½ c. minced onion
3 T. olive oil, divided
¼ c. minced green
  pepper
½ t. minced garlic
1 large ripe tomato,
  peeled, seeded,
  minced
¼ t. sugar
1 t. salt
freshly ground pepper
1 T. lemon juice

Put eggplant on rack in oven center; bake, turning once or twice, at 425° for 1 hour until inside is soft and skin chars and blisters. Remove skin; mash pulp and set aside. Saute onion in 2 tablespoons oil until soft. Stir in green pepper and garlic; cook for 5 minutes; add to mashed eggplant. Stir in tomato, sugar, salt and ground pepper. Heat remaining oil in a skillet; pour in eggplant mixture. Bring to a boil; simmer, covered, for 1 hour. Uncover and simmer, stirring occasionally, 30 minutes more until moisture evaporates and mixture thickens enough to hold shape in a spoon. Stir in lemon juice; correct seasonings. Refrigerate covered. Serve chilled with party bread.

Summit, New Providence, Berkeley Heights Welcome Wagon

Soups

Almond Bisque

Serves 6

¼ lb. salted almonds,
   unskinned (about 1 c.)
3 c. chicken broth
1 small onion, studded
   with cloves
1 bay leaf
2 T. butter
2 T. flour
½ c. hot milk
1 c. hot cream
chopped almonds or
   chives

Pulverize almonds in blender. Combine with broth, onion and bay leaf; simmer for 30 minutes. Discard onion and bay leaf. Keep mixture hot. Melt butter; stir in flour; cook over low heat, stirring constantly, until thick. Stir into soup. Cook over low heat for 5 minutes, stirring constantly. (Can be prepared in advance up to this point and refrigerated.) Stir in cream and milk; heat through. Do not allow soup to boil. Garnish with chopped almonds or chives.

Deanna Corona (Mrs. Joseph)

Broccoli Bisque

Serve 8

1¼-1½ lbs. fresh
   broccoli, cut into
   pieces
2 13¾ oz. cans chicken
   broth
1 medium onion,
   quartered
2 T. butter
1 t. salt
1-2 t. curry powder
pepper
1 T. lime juice
8 lemon slices
½ c. sour cream
1 T. chopped chives

Combine broccoli, broth, onion, butter, salt, curry powder and pepper. Bring to a boil; simmer, covered, for 8-12 minutes until tender. Blend mixture, a small amount at a time, in blender or food processor until smooth. Stir in lime juice; cover and chill. Garnish individual portions with lemon slice, sour cream, and chives.

Ann Low (Mrs. Calvin)

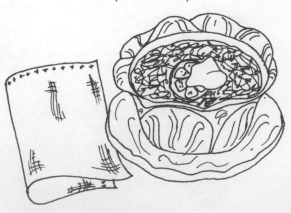

Black Bean Soup

Serves 6-8

2 c. dried black beans, rinsed
1 t. salt
2 c. chicken broth
1 c. chopped onion
1 t. chopped garlic
2 T. shortening
1 c. chopped cooked ham
1 large tomato, chopped
2 T. wine vinegar
½ t. ground cumin
¼ t. pepper

Simmer beans, salt and enough water to cover for 2½ hours until beans are tender; drain, reserving liquid. Add liquid to chicken broth to make 6 cups. Combine beans and broth; blend a small amount at a time in blender at high speed for 30 seconds. Saute onions and garlic in shortening for 5 minutes; add ham, tomato, vinegar, cumin and pepper; simmer, stirring frequently until thickened. Combine both mixtures; simmer 15 minutes.

Barbara Aaron (Mrs. Michael)

Senate Bean Soup

Yield: 4 quarts

1 lb. dried navy or pea beans, rinsed
water
1 meaty ham bone
3 medium potatoes, diced
1 large onion, chopped
1 c. diced celery
2 garlic cloves, minced
salt and pepper

In large kettle soak beans overnight in 2 quarts water. Next morning add 2 more quarts water. Add ham bone; bring to boil and skim. Cover; simmer 2 hours until beans begin to fall apart. Add remaining ingredients; simmer 1 hour. Remove ham from bone, chop and add to soup. To thicken, mash beans and potatoes against side of pan if desired. May be frozen.

Ann Newell (Mrs. Joseph)

Bulgarian Tarator

Serves 4

1 cucumber
½ t. salt
1 qt. yogurt
1 clove garlic, minced
1 c. water
2 T. oil
1 T. vinegar
½ c. chopped walnuts
2 T. finely chopped fresh dill

Peel and chop cucumber; add salt; let stand for 5-10 minutes. Combine remaining ingredients. Add cucumber. Salt and pepper to taste. Chill and serve with fresh crunchy bread or rolls.

Anny Schroeder (Mrs. Manfred)

Carrot Soup Granmère

Serves 8

6 onions
1½ lbs. fresh carrots
3 celery stalks
¼ c. chopped parsley
1 46 oz. can chicken
    broth
salt and pepper
sour creem
chopped chives

Cut onions, carrots and celery in coarse chunks. Combine with parsley, broth, salt and pepper; simmer, covered, until vegetables are very soft. Puree all ingredients in a blender. Heat; garnish each serving with a dollop of sour cream and a sprinkle of chives.

Mary Smith (Mrs. Albert C.)

Chicken Curry Soup with Fresh Fruit

Yield: 2 quarts

1¼ lb. chicken breast
6 c. chicken stock
¾ c. minced onion
¾ T. hot curry powder
⅝ c. canned tomatoes,
    drained, chopped
½ c. cubed, peeled apple
½ c. cubed banana
¼ c. raisins
¼ c. rice, uncooked
2 T. butter
¼ c. flour
¼ t. salt
½ c. heavy cream
freshly grated coconut,
    chopped salted
    peanuts or grated
    carrot

Cook chicken breast in stock 20 minutes until just tender. Remove chicken and reserve. Add next seven ingredients to stock; simmer 20 minutes until rice is done. Melt butter; stir in flour; cook roux over low heat, stirring for 3 minutes. Remove pan from heat. Add 1 cup of strained soup, whisking the mixture until smooth. Cook, stirring for 5 minutes. Stir into soup mixture. Simmer 5 minutes more. Bone and cut chicken into bite size pieces; add to soup with salt and cream. Garnish with coconut, peanuts or carrot.

The Essex County Soup Emporium, Montclair

Corn Chowder

Serves 4

2 ears fresh corn
2 pts. light cream
1½ pts. heavy cream
2 T. butter
1 packet instant chicken
    broth
salt and pepper

Barely cut tips of kernels off the cobs; scrape the rest of the corn off the cobs. Combine corn, creams, butter and instant broth; heat for 8 minutes.

Henry H. Hoyt, Jr.

Mushroom-Watercress Soup

Serves 12

2 c. mushrooms
2 onions, chopped
6 T. butter, melted
¼ c. flour
2½ qts. chicken or turkey
　stock
2 bunches watercress,
　chopped
salt and pepper

Chop mushroom stems and half of the caps. Add onions and chopped mushrooms to butter; cook covered until soft. Blend in flour; add 2 cups stock; cook, stirring, until thickened. Add remaining stock; simmer covered for 10-15 minutes. Thinly slice remaining mushroom caps; add to soup; simmer for 5 minutes. Add watercress and seasonings; simmer for 5-10 minutes.

Jane Rech (Mrs. William)

Mulligatawny Soup

Serves 6

¼ c. finely chopped
　onion
1½ t. curry powder
2 T. oil
1 tart apple, pared,
　chopped
¼ c. chopped carrots
¼ c. chopped celery
2 T. chopped green
　pepper
3 T. flour
4 c. chicken broth
1 16 oz. can tomatoes,
　chopped
1 T. chopped parsley
2 t. lemon juice
1 t. sugar
2 cloves
salt and pepper
1 c. diced cooked
　chicken

Saute onion and curry powder in oil until tender; add apple, carrot, celery and green pepper; cook for 5 minutes until vegetables are barely tender. Stir in flour; add broth, tomatoes, parsley, lemon juice, sugar, cloves, salt and pepper. Bring to a boil; add chicken; simmer for 30 minutes, stirring occasionally. (British and Scottish soldiers serving in India brought this curry-flavored soup back to England; thence to America with their descendents.)

Pera Simpson (Mrs. H.D.)

Cream of Onion Soup

3-4 onions, thinly sliced
3 T. butter, melted
2 T. flour
1 c. boiling water
1 qt. milk, scalded
½ c. evaporated milk,
    scalded
salt, pepper, paprika
Parmesan or Romano
    cheese

Cook onions in butter until golden; blend in flour. Add water gradually. Simmer, stirring constantly, until thickened and onions are tender. Add both milks; simmer for 10 minutes, stirring constantly. Add seasonings. Sprinkle individual portions with cheese.

Eleanor Pappky (Mrs. Herbert)

Fresh Tomato Soup

Serves 8

2 T. olive oil
¾ c. butter, divided
1 large onion, thinly
    sliced
2 sprigs fresh thyme
4 chopped basil leaves
salt and freshly ground
    pepper
2½ lbs. fresh tomatoes
3 T. tomato paste
¼ c. flour
3¾ c. chicken broth
1 t. sugar
1 c. heavy cream
croutons and chives

Heat olive oil with ½ cup butter in large pot. Add onion, thyme, basil, salt and pepper. Cook, stirring occasionally, until onion is wilted. Add tomatoes and tomato paste; stir to blend. Simmer 10 minutes. Place flour in small mixing bowl with 5 tablespoons broth, stirring to blend. Stir into tomato mixture; add remaining stock. Simmer 30 minutes, stirring frequently to prevent sticking. Put soup through fine sieve or food mill. Return to heat; add sugar and cream. Simmer about 5 minutes, stirring. Add remaining butter. Garnish with chives and sauteed croutons.

Pat Brown (Mrs. Phillip)

Cold Zucchini Soup

Serves 4

1 lb. zucchini, sliced
2 T. butter
2 T. diced onion
1 t. curry powder
½ t. salt
1 13 oz. can chicken
    broth
½ c. heavy cream

Saute zucchini and onion in butter until soft. Process in blender; add remaining ingredients; blend until smooth. Serve chilled.

Jessie Hassell (Mrs. Arthur)

Lentil Soup

3 c. diced cooked ham
½ lb. kielbasa, sliced
2 onions, chopped
⅛ t. instant minced garlic
¼ c. oil
2 c. chopped celery with
   leaves
1 16 oz. can tomatoes,
   drained, chopped
1 lb. lentils
3 qts. water
½ t. hot red pepper sauce
1½ t. salt

In large soup kettle or saucepan, saute ham, kielbasa, onions and garlic in oil for 5 minutes. Add remaining ingredients and simmer for 2 hours.

Lee Swenson (Mrs. C. Richard)

Strawberry and Wine Soup

2 c. strawberries
1 c. water
½ c. sugar
1 c. Chablis
½ t. lemon juice
1 t. grated lemon peel
½ c. pearl tapioca,
   cooked
strawberries, sliced

Blend strawberries, water and sugar in blender until pureed. Blend in wine, lemon juice and lemon peel. Stir in tapioca. Chill. Garnish individual portions with sliced strawberries.

Ruth Layng (Mrs. E.T.)

Shrimp Soup

4 c. water
½ t. salt
1 bay leaf
½ lb. small fresh shrimp
1 medium onion, minced
2 T. olive oil
2 t. paprika
2 T. butter, melted
2 T. flour
salt and pepper
2-3 T. light dry Port wine
croutons

Bring water, salt and bay leaf to a boil; add shrimp. Simmer for 2-5 minutes; drain, reserving liquid. Shell shrimp, reserving shells. Saute onion in oil; add paprika and shrimp shells. Cook, stirring, over low heat for a few minutes. Combine butter and flour to make a smooth paste; gradually add reserved liquid. Cook, stirring, to a smooth sauce. Add sauce to onion mixture; heat, stirring occasionally for 5 minutes. Strain into a large kettle; add shrimp. Heat through; season with salt, pepper and wine. Garnish individual portions with croutons.

Peggy Chussler

Shrimp Gazpacho

1 garlic clove, split
10 oz. tiny shrimp, cooked
6 T. lemon juice
3 c. chopped fresh tomatoes
2 c. tomato juice
½ c. chopped green pepper
½ c. chopped onion
¼ c. minced parsley
2 c. chopped cucumber
2 T. minced chives
2-3 t. salt
Tabasco
⅓ c. olive oil
¼-½ t. ground cumin (optional)

Rub a large wooden bowl with garlic clove. Place shrimp in bowl; sprinkle with lemon juice. Add remaining ingredients and chill overnight.

Alicia Branch (Mrs. Elmer)

Italian Wedding Soup

1 lb. ground beef
1 c. bread crumbs
⅓ c. Parmesan or
   Romano cheese
2 eggs, beaten
chopped parsley
garlic powder
salt and pepper
2 large cans chicken
   broth
1 bunch celery, chopped
2 lbs. endive, chopped
diced cooked chicken
noodles

Combine beef, crumbs, grated cheese, eggs, parsley and seasonings; form in walnut-sized balls. Add to heated broth; simmer for 3 minutes. Add celery and endive; cook until flavors are blended. Add chicken and noodles; simmer until noodles are tender.

Janice Stowell (Mrs. Edward)

Salads

Asparagus and Potato Salad

Serves 6

1 c. oil
⅓ c. wine vinegar
½ c. sliced scallions
1 T. dill
1 T. Dijon mustard
salt and pepper
2 lbs. new potatoes,
    cooked, sliced
2 lbs. asparagus,
    cooked

Combine first 6 ingredients; toss with potatoes. Refrigerate overnight. To serve, arrange asparagus in spoke fashion. Mound potatoes in center; pour remaining dressing over asparagus.

Brenda MacDowell (Mrs. David)

Artichoke and Chick-Pea Salad

Serves 4

1 garlic clove, minced
2 T. lemon juice
½ t. salt
½ t. oregano
¼ t. crushed red pepper
1 6 oz. jar marinated
    artichoke hearts
1 10 oz. can chick-peas,
    drained
½ c. small pimiento-
    stuffed olives

Stir together garlic, lemon juice, salt, oregano and pepper until blended. Add remaining ingredients; toss to mix. Serve chilled.

Charlanne Lamberto (Mrs. Victor)

Stuffed Avocado

Serves 2

1 ripe avacado, halved,
    peeled
6 oz. Swiss cheese cut
    in ½″ strips
½ c. diced celery
2 T. sour cream
salt, pepper
1 T. lemon juice
pitted black olives

Mix cheese, celery, sour cream and seasoning. Sprinkle avocado halves with lemon juice. Add filling. Garnish with olives.

Maryalice Marakas (Mrs. James)

Marinated Broccoli-Mushroom Salad

Serves 4-6

1 lb. fresh mushrooms, sliced
1 bunch fresh broccoli flowerets
1 bottle Herb-Garlic dressing
1 pt. cherry tomatoes

Marinate mushrooms and brocoli in dressing for 24 hours. Two to eight hours before serving, add tomatoes. Season if desired. Drain before serving. Dressing may be used again.

Doris Petersen (Mrs. Richard)

Tangy Cauliflower Salad

Serves 6

1 medium cauliflower
3 carrots, shredded
½ c. salad dressing, Italian or French
1 avocado
½ c. sliced Spanish olives
¼ c. Roquefort cheese, crumbled

Separate cauliflower into flowerets; slice into bite-size pieces; add carrots. Marinate in dressing for 1 hour. Before serving, dice avocado and add with olives and cheese. Toss lightly.

Pi Beta Phi Alumnae Club of Northern New Jersey

Cauliflower-Apple Salad

Serves 6-8

1 small head cauliflower, thinly sliced
3 red apples, unpeeled, diced
1 c. sliced celery
3 small green scallions, sliced
¾ c. chopped parsley or 1 small bunch watercress, chopped
½ t. salt
¼ c. red wine vinegar
¼ c. salad oil
pepper

Combine all ingredients.

Carolyn Nicholson (Mrs. Ralph)

Cucumber Salad

1 c. sour cream
4 whole scallions, chopped
½ green pepper, chopped
1 garlic clove, crushed in press
1½ t. salt
½ t. pepper
1½ t. paprika
1 t. sugar
½ c. wine vinegar
2 large cucumbers, peeled, thinly sliced
fresh parsley

Combine all ingredients except cucumber and parsley. Add cucumbers; chill until serving time. Garnish with parsley. (Can be made the day before.)

Lynn Kiefer (Mrs. Raymond)

Tomartichokes

6 large tomatoes
6 canned artichokes
salt, pepper
dill
⅓ c. mayonnaise
⅓ c. sour cream
1 T. lemon juice
½ t. curry powder

Skin tomatoes, slice off tops; scoop out seeds and some of the pulp. Drain upside down. Season inside with salt, pepper and dill. Place one artichoke in each tomato. Chill. Combine remaining ingredients. Spoon over tomatoes.

Brenda MacDowell (Mrs. David)

Fall Salad with Coriander Dressing

6 T. salad oil
3 T. lemon juice
½ t. dried mustard
½ t. ground coriander
¼ t. salt
¼ t. sugar
⅛ t. pepper
1 head Boston lettuce
1 can artichoke hearts, quartered
2 c. grapes
1 small knob fennel, thinly sliced

Combine oil, lemon juice and seasonings. Set aside. Line salad bowl with lettuce. Combine artichoke hearts, grapes and fennel with dressing; add to salad bowl and serve.

Penny Peniston

Mostly Mushroom Salad

Serves 6

1 lb. fresh mushrooms,
  sliced
1 c. diced celery
1 c. diced green pepper
2 T. finely chopped
  onion
2 T. olive oil
1 T. wine vinegar
2 t. salt
⅛ t. freshly ground black
  pepper
2 T. lemon juice

Place mushrooms, celery, green pepper and onion in a salad bowl. Combine remaining ingredients; pour over vegetables, tossing gently. Serve immediately. (59 calories per portion)

Diantha Pearson (Mrs. Earle)

Red-Tipped Lettuce Salad with Poppy Seed Dressing

Serves 4

1-2 avocados, sliced
2 small cans mandarin
   oranges, drained
1 cucumber, peeled,
   sliced
red-tipped leaf lettuce
red onion, sliced,
   separated into rings

Dressing:
⅓ c. sugar
1 t. dry mustard
1 t. salt
⅓ c. cider vinegar
1 c. salad oil
1½ T. poppy seeds
1 T. onion juice or
  minced onion

Arrange salad ingredients in large serving bowl. Blend dressing ingredients slowly in blender. Toss and serve. (You will not need to use all the dressing unless it is a very large salad.)

Nancy Brink (Mrs. Ronald)

43

German Potato Salad

Serves 8-10

8 slices bacon
2 T. cornstarch
1 c. vinegar
1 c. water
½ c. sugar
salt, pepper
dry mustard
2 lbs. potatoes, cooked,
   peeled, sliced
2 eggs, hard-cooked,
   sliced
¼ c. chopped onion or
   scallions
½ c. chopped celery

Cook and crumble bacon, reserving grease. To the bacon grease add cornstarch, vinegar, water, sugar, salt, pepper and mustard. Bring to a boil. Pour over potatoes. Add remaining ingredients. Serve warm.

Grace Bollenbacher (Mrs. John)

Spinach Salad One

Serves 4

½ lb. fresh spinach
¼ lb. fresh mushrooms,
   sliced
1 c. fresh bean sprouts
1 hard-cooked egg,
   chopped
1 small onion, chopped
croutons
crisp bacon, crumbled

Piquant Dressing:
3-4 T. soy sauce
2 T. vinegar
2 T. vegetable oil
1 t. onion, minced
½ t. sugar
¼ t. pepper

Toss spinach, mushrooms, bean sprouts, egg and onion together. Add Piquant Dressing and toss again. Top with croutons and bacon.

Dressing: Place ingredients in a jar and shake to blend.

Jane Bischoff (Mrs. Barton)
Anne Jamison (Mrs. R. Barnett, Jr.)

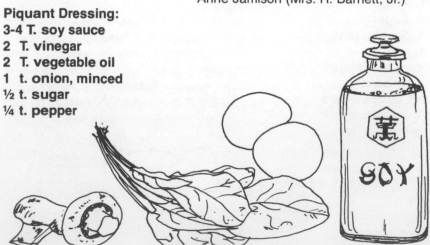

Spinach Salad Two

1 lb. spinach
⅔ c. croutons
5 T. butter
2 stalks celery, sliced
8 ripe olives, pitted, sliced
1 medium red onion, sliced
2 medium tomatoes, cut in wedges
2 hard-boiled eggs

Roquefort Dressing:
1 c. sour cream
1 c. mayonnaise
2 t. finely chopped onion
½ t. Worcestershire sauce
⅛ t. garlic salt
½ t. freshly ground black pepper
¼ t. cayenne pepper
2 t. sugar
2-3 oz. Roquefort cheese, crumbled

Saute croutons with butter for 10-15 minutes until golden brown and crisp. Keep all ingredients separate until ready to serve. Toss with Roquefort Dressing. Garnish with wedges of tomato and hard-boiled egg pressed through a sieve.

Dressing: Combine all ingredients. (Best made a day ahead. Also good as a dip.)

Jane C. Rech (Mrs. William)

Berry's Salad

Serves 6-8

2 bunches fresh spinach, washed, dried
1 pt. fresh strawberries, washed, hulled, halved
½ c. sugar
2 T. sesame seeds
1 T. poppy seeds
1½ t. minced onion
¼ t. Worcestershire sauce
¼ t. paprika
½ c. oil
¼ c. vinegar

Arrange spinach and strawberries attractively on individual serving plates. Place next six ingredients in blender. With blender running, add oil and vinegar in slow steady stream until thoroughly mixed and thickened. Drizzle over berries and spinach. Serve immediately.

Kathy Diaz (Mrs. Israel)

Molded Spinach Salad

Serves 8

1 pkg. lemon gelatin
1 c. boiling water
½ c. cold water
½ T. vinegar or 2 T. lemon juice
½ c. mayonnaise
salt and pepper
1 c. chopped fresh spinach
⅓ c. diced celery
¾ c. small curd cottage cheese
1 T. finely chopped onion
2 T. grated carrot (optional)

Dissolve gelatin in boiling water. Add cold water, vinegar or lemon juice, mayonnaise, salt and pepper. Beat with electric mixer. Chill until partially set. Beat again until fluffy. Fold in remaining ingredients. Pour into greased 2½ quart mold. Chill until set.

Pam Bess (Mrs. Stanley)
Pi Beta Phi Alumnae Club of Northern New Jersey

Frosted Polynesian Salad

Serves 12-16

1 small head iceburg lettuce, shredded
1 10 oz. pkg. frozen peas, cooked
2 medium green peppers, diced
1 medium red onion, thinly sliced
2 8 oz. cans water chestnuts, thinly sliced
2 15 oz. cans pineapple tidbits, drained
2 4 oz. cans sliced mushrooms, drained
1½ c. mayonnaise
1½ c. sour cream
5 T. sugar
¾ lb. Cheddar cheese, grated
¾ lb. fried bacon, crumbled

Line a 3 quart glass salad bowl with shredded lettuce. Layer vegetables and pineapple in dish. Combine mayonnaise, sour cream and sugar; use to frost vegetables. Cover and chill overnight. Two hours before serving, sprinkle with bacon and cheese.

Ruth Smith (Mrs. Sheridan)

Molded Reuben Salad

2 3 oz. pkgs. lemon
   gelatin
1 c. boiling tomato juice
1 c. cold water, divided
2 c. sauerkraut, drained,
   chopped
1 t. caraway seed
1 c. shredded Swiss
   cheese
1 c. boiling water
3 T. Thousand Island
   dressing
1 12 oz. can corned
   beef, chopped
¼ c. minced green onion
salad greens
pickles

Dissolve one package gelatin in tomato juice. Stir in ½ cup cold water. Chill until slightly thickened; fold in sauerkraut and caraway seed. Turn into lightly greased 13x9″ pan. Sprinkle cheese evenly over gelatin. Chill. Dissolve remaining gelatin in 1 cup boiling water; stir in ½ cup cold water. Chill until slightly thickened. Blend in dressing, corned beef and onion. Spread over cheese; chill until firm. Cut into 3″ squares; serve on greens. Garnish with pickles and additional Thousand Island dressing, if desired.

Carolyn Walters

Taco Salad

1 lb. ground beef,
   cooked
¼ t. cumin
salt
half-head of lettuce,
   shredded
2 onions, chopped
1½ c. grated Cheddar
   cheese
1½ c. chopped, peeled
   tomatoes
12 sliced ripe olives
taco-flavored tortilla
   chips, broken
7½ oz. mild taco sauce

Mix ground beef with cumin and salt. Chill. Toss with all other ingredients. If layered ahead, add lettuce, tortilla chips, and taco sauce just before tossing to serve.

Jane Rech (Mrs. William)

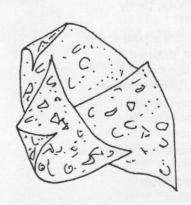

Fresh Vegetable Salad

Serves 6

1½ c. cherry tomatoes, halved
1½ c. each thinly sliced mushrooms, zucchini, carrots, green onions, green pepper rings
1½ c. broccoli flowerets
1½ c. cauliflowerets
1 garlic clove, halved
1 t. salt
½ t. dry mustard
½ t. ground pepper
1 t. chopped chives
2 T. red wine vinegar
1 T. lemon juice
2 T. olive oil
watercress
spinach leaves

Prepare vegetables; set aside. Rub salad bowl with cut garlic. Put vegetables into bowl. Combine next seven ingredients in a jar; cover; shake for 30 seconds. Pour over vegetables; cover; marinate for at least 2 hours in refrigerator. Drain; serve with watercress and spinach leaves.

Pi Beta Phi Alumnae Club of Northern New Jersey

Rainbow Vegetable Platter

Serves 10

2 pkg. frozen baby lima beans
½ T. dill
Wishbone Italian Dressing
8 small zucchini
½ c. Parmesan cheese
2 pkg. frozen sugar-glazed carrots
½ c. wine vinegar
2 pkg. frozen asparagus spears
½ c. capers with liquid
3-4 tomatoes, sliced

French dressing:
½ c. sour cream
1 T. lemon juice
½ c. mayonnaise
salt, pepper
chopped parsley

Cook each vegetable individually (zucchini, 3 minutes until still crisp); drain. Marinate the following overnight: lima beans with dill and Italian dressing, carrots with vinegar. Toss zucchini with cheese. Toss asparagus with capers. Arrange on platter with sliced tomatoes. Drizzle with French dressing; serve remainder in bowl.

Helen Hanson (Mrs. James)

Rice Salad

cooked long grain rice
cooked mushrooms,
   sliced
celery, finely sliced
scallions, finely sliced
mixed vegetables,
   cooked (frozen corn,
   peas, beans)
green and red peppers,
   diced
tomato, diced
green and black olives,
   sliced
vinaigrette dressing

Mix all ingredients with dressing. Serve with cold cuts. (Try to make the salad as colorful as possible.)

Patricia Ellis (Mrs. Roy)

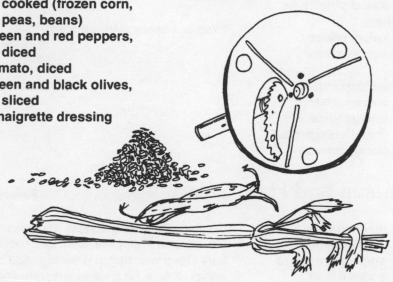

Rice-Ham Salad

Serves 10

1½ c. long grain rice
¼ c. French dressing
5 oz. peas
¾ c. mayonnaise
1 T. chopped green
   onion
½ t. salt
½-1 t. curry powder
½ t. dry mustard
pepper
1 c. raw cauliflower, cut
   into flowerets
½ c. chopped celery
½ c. sliced radishes
8 oz. ham, julienned

Cook rice; toss with French dressing and chill. Cook peas and chill. Combine remaining ingredients except vegetables and ham. Add to rice. Add vegetables and ham.

Kay Shea (Mrs. John)

Western Ham Salad

Serves 8

1   head lettuce
2   c. julienne strips of
     ham
1   c. orange or mandarin
     orange segments
2½ c. pineapple chunks
1   c. sliced pitted ripe
     olives
1   c. celery slices
1   avocado, sliced

Orange Mayonnaise:
1   c. mayonnaise
¼   c. orange juice
½   t. grated orange peel
1   t. orange liqueur

Have all ingredients chilled. Tear lettuce into bite-sized pieces in a bowl. Add all other ingredients. Drizzle with Orange Mayonnaise.

Orange Mayonnaise: Blend all ingredients.

Eleanor Pappky (Mrs. Herbert)

Banana and Ham Salad

Serves 4

½   c. mayonnaise
½   c. sour cream
1   T. prepared mustard
1   t. grated onion
2   T. lemon juice
¼   t. salt
⅛   t. hot pepper sauce
2   T. chopped parsley
1   lb. cooked ham, cubed
2   c. chopped, pared
     cucumber
2   bananas, sliced
salad greens

Combine first 8 ingredients for dressing. Cover; chill. Combine ham and cucumbers. Toss with half of dressing. Add bananas. Serve on greens with remaining dressing.

June Riley (Mrs. W.H.)

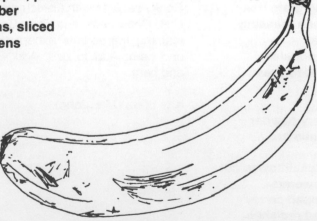

Cranberry Wine Salad

Serves 10-12

**2 3 oz. pkgs. raspberry
gelatin
2 c. boiling water
1 16 oz. can whole
cranberry sauce
1 8¾ oz. can crushed
pineapple, undrained
¾ c. port wine
¼ c. chopped walnuts**

Dissolve gelatin in boiling water. Stir in all ingredients except walnuts. Chill until partially set. Fold in nuts. Pour into greased 6½ cup mold. Chill until set.

Fran Denecke (Mrs. Olin)

Pineapple-Walnut Mold

Serves 10-12

**2 envelopes unflavored
gelatin
½ c. cold water
2½ c. crushed
pineapple, undrained
3 T. lemon juice
½ c. sugar
1 c. heavy cream,
whipped
1 c. shredded Cheddar
cheese
2 c. chopped walnuts
walnut halves**

Soften gelatin in cold water. Heat pineapple; stir in softened gelatin until dissolved. Add lemon juice and sugar; chill until partially set. Fold in whipped cream, cheese, and nuts. Pour into greased 6 cup mold; chill until set. Unmold; garnish with walnut halves.

Lisa Gibson (Mrs. John)

Healthy Fruit Salad

¾ c. roasted unsalted
   nuts, chopped
½-1 c. roasted
   sunflower seeds
3 bananas, sliced
1 c. fresh or canned
   sliced peaches
½ c. shredded coconut
1 c. grapes
3 apples, sliced,
   unpeeled
½ c. orange segments
2 t. grated orange rind
½ c. raisins
2 T. honey
½ c. dry white wine or 2
   T. sweet sherry
fresh mint leaves,
   chopped (reserve
   some for garnish)
sour cream, yogurt or
   cream

Place all ingredients in large bowl. Chill.
Serve with sour cream, yogurt, or cream.

Jean McDonnell (Mrs. John)

Fruit Fluff

Yield: 3 cups dressing

sliced pears
quartered peaches
whole strawberries
grapes
sweet cherries
blueberries

Dressing:
1 small pkg. instant
   vanilla pudding
2 c. cold milk
1 c. sour cream
1 t. grated orange peel
¼ c. orange juice

Beat pudding mix with milk until well
blended, 1-2 minutes. Gently fold in sour
cream, orange peel and juice. Chill. To
serve, place small bowl of dressing in
large shallow bowl with fruits arranged
around it.

The Committee

Bacon Dressing

¾ c. olive oil
¼ c. white wine vinegar
juice of 1 lemon
½ t. Accent
¼ t. paprika
½ t. salt
3 T. bacon grease

Combine all ingredients. (Good with spinach salad, garnished with hard-cooked egg and bacon.)

Katherine Senn (Mrs. Laurence)

Homemade Blue Cheese Dressing

Yield: 2½ cups

1 c. Miracle Whip salad dressing
1 c. buttermilk
1 t. garlic salt
1 T. Worcestershire sauce
8 oz. blue cheese, divided
1 T. sour cream

Combine 4 ounces of the blue cheese with remaining ingredients in blender at low speed. Pour into refrigerator jar; add remaining crumbled blue cheese. Shake. Store in refrigerator.

Jacquelyn Marvin (Mrs. William)

Paige's Salad Dressing

Yield: ⅓ cup

2 T. olive oil
2 T. mayonnaise
1½ t. Dijon mustard
2½ t. wine vinegar

To the olive oil, add the rest of the ingredients. Blend well.

Paige von Hoffmann

Dog Team French Dressing

⅓ c. sugar
1 T. dry mustard
1 t. salt
1 t. basil
1 t. marjoram
1 mashed garlic clove
½ c. salad oil
½ c. cider vinegar

Combine all ingredients.

Bobbie Tooher (Mrs. James)

Curry Chablis Dressing

Yield: 1 cup

⅔ c. salad oil
¼ c. white vinegar
2 T. Chablis or dry
   vermouth
2 t. soy sauce
1 t. sugar
1 t. dry mustard
½ t. salt
½ t. garlic salt
¼-1 t. curry powder

Combine all ingredients in jar. Shake well.

Karen Cooper (Mrs. Charles)
Janice Stowell (Mrs. Edward)

Shallot Dressing

Yield: 1 cup

½ c. vegetable oil
2 T. olive oil
2 T. tarragon vinegar
1 t. sugar
1½ t. honey
3 shallots, peeled,
   chopped
3 sprigs parsley
1 T. Dijon mustard
2 T. soy sauce

Put all ingredients in blender; blend for 40 seconds. Chill until ready to serve.

Joan Stettler (Mrs. Wayne)

Tomato Soup Dressing

1 can tomato soup
1 c. oil
½ c. vinegar
2 T. sugar
1 t. dry mustard
1 T. Worcestershire
   sauce
1 t. parsley
1 T. chopped onion
1 garlic clove
1 t. paprika
salt and pepper

Shake all together.

Hank Kleckner (Mrs. Donald)

54

Vinaigrette Salad Dressing

1   c. vegetable oil
⅓ c. vinegar
1   garlic clove, crushed
2   T. fresh or dried dill, chopped
1   t. horseradish
salt, pepper, thyme

Combine all ingredients in jar and shake to mix. Refrigerate to chill.

Peter Lebovitz

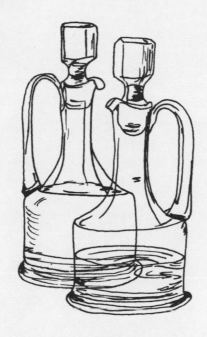

Beef

Hamburger au Poivre

Serves 6

2 lbs. ground beef
1 T. freshly ground black pepper, divided
6 1" slices French bread
3 T. butter, divided
½ c. red wine
1 t. instant beef bouillon

Shape beef into 6 half-inch thick oval patties. Sprinkle ¼ teaspoon pepper on each side of patty. Saute bread in 2 tablespoons butter until golden brown on both sides. Remove; keep warm. Cook patties in same pan for 3 minutes per side. Add wine; cook, covered, over medium heat for 3 minutes. Lift patties onto bread slices. Add bouillon to pan drippings with remaining butter, stirring constantly until it thickens slightly. Pour over patties.

Cindy Kellog (Mrs. William)

Stuffed Burger Bundles

Serves 5

⅓ c. evaporated milk
1 lb. ground beef
1 c. herb-seasoned stuffing mix, prepared according to pkg. directions
1 can cream of mushroom soup
2 t. Worcestershire sauce
1 T. ketchup

Combine milk and beef; shape into 5 6-inch patties. Place ¼ cup stuffing in center of each; pull sides of patties up to cover stuffing and seal. Place in a 1½ quart baking dish. Combine soup, Worcestershire sauce and ketchup; pour over burger bundles. Bake uncovered at 350° for 35-40 minutes.

Pam Bess (Mrs. Stanley)

Sweet and Sour Meatballs

Serves 8

1 16 oz. can sauerkraut
1 16 oz. can tomatoes
1 4 oz. can tomato sauce
1 c. brown sugar
½ c. sugar
½ c. lemon juice
2 lbs. ground beef
2 eggs, beaten
¼ c. milk
1 t. garlic salt
12 gingersnaps, crushed

Blend sauerkraut, tomatoes, tomato sauce, sugars, and lemon juice in blender until smooth. Bring to a boil. Combine beef, eggs, milk and garlic salt; form into meatballs. Simmer in sauce for 45 minutes. Add gingersnaps; simmer for 15 minutes.

Rita Weinberg (Mrs. Abby)

Beef and Beans Supreme

Serves 14-16

1 lb. ground beef
½ lb. bacon, cut into pieces
1 c. chopped onions
½ c. ketchup
½ t. salt
¼ t. seasoned salt
½ c. sugar
½ c. brown sugar
1 t. dry mustard
2 t. vinegar
8 drops Tabasco
2 15 oz. cans pork and beans, undrained
1 15 oz. can kidney beans, undrained
1 15 oz. can butter beans, undrained

Saute beef, bacon and onion until beef is browned; drain. Add remaining ingredients; turn into an ovenproof casserole. Bake at 350° for 1 hour or longer until most of the liquid is absorbed.

Phyllis Schroeder (Mrs. Edward)

Heavenly Hash

Serves 12

2½ lbs. ground beef
2 onions, chopped
1 large green pepper, chopped
1 T. salt
1 lb. mushrooms, sliced
¼ lb. butter
½ t. salt
8 oz. medium noodles, cooked
2 cans tomato soup
1 6 oz. can tomato paste
2 6 oz. cans bean sprouts, drained
2 T. Worcestershire sauce
½ lb. sharp Cheddar cheese, grated

Saute meat, onions, green pepper and salt. Saute mushrooms in butter and salt. Combine all ingredients, except cheese, in a greased casserole. Sprinkle cheese on top. Bake at 300° for 1 hour covered and ½ hour uncovered.

Gini Bowers (Mrs. J. Donald)

Grecian Beef and Macaroni

Serves 6-8

1½ lbs. ground beef
½ t. cinnamon
salt and pepper
1 8 oz. can tomato sauce
1 c. chicken broth
1 cinnamon stick
2 T. butter
¾ lb. macaroni, cooked
½ c. grated magetha or
   Romano cheese

Saute beef; season with cinnamon, salt and pepper. Simmer tomato sauce, broth, cinnamon stick and butter until slightly thickened; reserve half of the sauce. Layer macaroni, beef, cheese and sauce in ovenproof serving dish until all ingredients are used, ending with a layer of beef. Sprinkle with cheese. Bake at 325° for 30 minutes. Reheat reserved sauce; spoon over individual servings.

Maryalice Marakas (Mrs. James)

South African Babute

Serves 8

2 lbs. lean ground beef
salt
1½ T. curry powder
4 eggs, beaten
1 c. milk
1½ c. half and half
1 8 oz. pkg. dried
   apricots, finely
   chopped
bay leaves
butter

Combine beef, salt and curry powder. Combine eggs, milk and cream. Combine half of the egg mixture with the beef; stir in apricots. Turn into a greased 13x9" baking dish. Pour remaining egg mixture over top; float several bay leaves on top of milk; dot with butter. Bake at 350° for 45 minutes until top resembles baked custard.

Ruth McKinley (Mrs. Gordon)

Sicilian Meat Loaf

Serves 8

2 eggs, beaten
¾ c. soft bread crumbs
½ c. tomato juice
3 T. chopped parsley
½ t. oregano
¼ t. salt
¼ t. pepper
1 garlic clove, minced
2 lbs. ground beef
8 slices Italian ham
1½ c. shredded
   mozzarella cheese
mozzarella cheese slices

Combine eggs, crumbs, tomato juice, parsley, oregano, salt, pepper, garlic and beef. On waxed paper, shape meat into a 10 x 12" rectangle. Place ham on top, leaving small margin around edges. Sprinkle with cheese. Starting with short end, roll up meat, sealing edges and ends. Place seam side down in 9 x 13 pan. Bake at 350° for 1 hour. Place cheese slices over top of roll; bake for 5 minutes until cheese melts.

Lynne Tully (Mrs. Paul)

Hungry Boys' Casserole

Serves 6-8

1½ lbs. ground beef
1 c. chopped celery
½ c. chopped onion
½ c. chopped green
   pepper
1 garlic clove, minced
1 6 oz. can tomato paste
¾ c. water
½ t. salt
½ t. monosodium
   glutimate
1 t. paprika
1 16 oz. can pork and
   beans, undrained
1 16 oz. can chick peas,
   drained
1 pkg. refrigerator
   biscuits
2 T. sliced green olives
1 T. slivered almonds

Combine beef, celery, onion, pepper and garlic. Saute until beef is browned and vegetables are tender; drain. Add remaining ingredients except biscuits, olives and almonds; simmer 5-10 minutes. Reserve 1 cup of the meat mixture; pour remaining into a greased 13x9" baking dish. With cookie cutter, cut a hole in each biscuit, reserving holes; arrange biscuit rings on top of meat. Combine olives and almonds with reserved meat mixture; spoon into biscuit ring centers. Top with biscuit holes. Bake at 425° for 15-20 minutes until browned.

Kay Plossl (Mrs. William)

Skid Row Stroganoff

Serves 4

½ c. chopped onion
1½ lbs. ground beef
2 T. butter
½ lb. mushrooms, sliced,
   sauteed in butter or 2
   4 oz. cans sliced
   mushrooms
3 T. dry red wine
3 T. lemon juice
1 can beef bouillon
salt and pepper
2 c. thin noodles
1 c. sour cream

Brown onions and beef in butter; drain off fat. Add mushrooms, wine, lemon juice, bouillon, salt and pepper. Lay noodles on top. Simmer, covered, for 30 minutes. Stir in sour cream; heat through.

Betty Kipp (Mrs. Donald)

Taco Pie

Serves 4

1 pkg. refrigerated
   crescent rolls or 1 9″
   pie shell, unbaked
2 c. corn chips, crushed,
   divided
1 lb. ground beef,
   browned, drained
1 pkg. taco seasoning
   mix
½ c. water
1 c. sour cream
1½-2 c. grated Cheddar
   cheese
chopped lettuce, onion,
   tomatoes

Press crescent roll dough on bottom and sides of a greased 9″ pie plate; cover bottom of crust with half of the chips. Combine beef, taco mix and water; simmer 15-20 minutes. Pour meat on top of chips; spread with sour cream. Sprinkle with cheese; top with remaining chips. Bake at 375° for 20-30 minutes; cool 5 minutes before cutting. Top with lettuce, onion, tomatoes and cheese.

Jane Persons (Mrs. James)

Barbecued Beef for Sandwiches

Serves 12-15

1 3 lb. beef chuck roast,
   browned
2 c. beef bouillon
2 large onions, chopped
1 c. chili sauce
½ c. vinegar
½ c. water
1 T. chili powder
1 T. butter
½ t. salt
¼ t. pepper
basil
thyme
½ t. garlic salt
2 t. sugar
12-15 hamburger buns

Cook roast in bouillon and onions until tender; cool. Cut or tear meat into small pieces. Chill pan juices; skim off fat. Combine remaining ingredients except buns; add to meat juices. Thicken with mixture of flour and water. Add meat. Spoon into buns.

Ann Newell (Mrs. Joseph)

Sauerbraten

1 4 lb. bottom round of beef
1½ c. water
1½ c. cider or wine vinegar
2 onions, sliced
3 bay leaves
6 celery tops, chopped
12 peppercorns
1 large carrot, quartered
¼ t. thyme
4 cloves
flour
salt and pepper
2 T. oil
⅓ c. seedless raisins, plumped in boiling water
5 gingersnaps, crushed

Marinate beef in combined water, vinegar, onions, bay leaves, celery, peppercorns, carrot, thyme and cloves in refrigerator, covered, for 2 days, turning twice daily. Drain, reserving liquid. Lightly dredge in seasoned flour; brown quickly on all sides in oil. Add marinade; simmer covered for 3 hours until tender, adding water if necessary. Remove meat from marinade; chill; slice. Puree marinade in blender; add raisins and gingersnaps; heat. Add beef; heat thoroughly.

Jeanne Keyes (Mrs. William)

Bar-B-Q Beef

Serves 8

1 4 lb. rolled rump or top sirloin of beef
flour
salt and pepper
2 T. horseradish
1 c. water
½ c. vinegar
1 bay leaf
oregano
2 large onions, minced
¼ t. pepper
1 26 oz. bottle ketchup
3 T. sugar
1 green pepper, sliced

Dredge beef in seasoned flour. Roast at 325° for 1¼ hours; spread top with horseradish; roast for an additional hour. Reduce temperature to 300°. Combine water, vinegar, bay leaf, oregano, onions, pepper, ketchup and sugar. Baste beef with ½ cup of sauce every 15 minutes until all is used. Turn off oven; leave beef in oven for 1 hour. Place green pepper over beef; refrigerate, covered, overnight. To serve, slice thinly and reheat beef in sauce.

Priscilla Haberstroh (Mrs. Donald)

Beef Napoli

1 4 lb. eye-round or
  sirloin roast of beef
1 5 oz. stick of
  pepperoni
1 can beef bouillon
¼ c. vinegar
2 drops red-pepper
  seasoning
4 T. flour
½ c. water
1 T. brown sugar

Stand roast on end; cut a small "X" through center; stuff hole with pepperoni. Brown on all sides in oil; drain off fat. Add bouillon, vinegar and red pepper seasoning. Simmer, covered, for 3 hours until tender, turning several times. Remove to serving platter; keep warm. Heat pan liquid to boiling; thicken with mixture of flour and water, stirring in sugar. Pour over sliced meat.

Nancy Morrow (Mrs. David)

Italian Crock Pot Roast

Serves 6-8

3-4 lb. pot roast
3 potatoes, peeled,
  sliced
3 carrots, sliced
2 onions, sliced
½ c. beef consomme
salt and pepper
1 8 oz. can tomato
  sauce
1 t. oregano
1 t. basil

Put all vegetables and seasonings in crock pot. Salt and pepper the roast and place on top of vegetables. Add consomme. Cover and cook on low setting for 10-12 hours, or high setting for 4-5 hours. Remove meat; slice and serve with vegetables. (Variation: omit tomato sauce, oregano and basil. Add four dill pickles and 1 teaspoon dill.)

Joseph I. Boylan, Jr., M.D.

Coffee Pot Roast

Serves 6

1 3½ lb. rolled beef pot
  roast
flour
salt and pepper
3 T. butter
1 c. strong coffee
½ c. bourbon
1 c. canned cranberry
  sauce
2 T. flour
2 T. butter
3 T. chopped parsley

Dredge meat with seasoned flour; brown on all sides in butter; pour off drippings. Add coffee, bourbon, and cranberry sauce. Simmer for 3 hours until tender, turning once after 1½ hours. Combine flour and butter; stir into pan liquid. Cook, stirring, until thickened. Pour over sliced meat; sprinkle with parsley.

Ruthelizabeth Lovretin (Mrs. Andrew)

Easy Beef Burgundy

Serves 6-8

2 lbs. beef, cubed
flour
salt and pepper
1 can tomato
  bisque soup
1 can onion soup
½ c. dry red wine
8 oz. fresh mushrooms,
  sliced

Dredge beef in flour, salt and pepper. Place in ovenproof casserole; add soups. Bake, covered, at 300° for 2½ hours. Add wine and mushrooms; bake for 30 minutes. Serve over rice.

Doris Calvert (Mrs. William)

Hunter Stew

Serves 6

2 lbs. beef chuck, cubed
2 large onions,
  quartered
2 garlic cloves, minced
3 T. oil
1 T. flour
2 16 oz. cans stewed
  tomatoes
1 6 oz. can tomato paste
1 t. chili powder
1 t. oregano
½ t. rosemary
1½ t. seasoned salt
½ c. chopped parsley
½ c. water
3 carrots, sliced 1" thick
½ lb. ziti, cooked
⅓ c. Parmesan cheese

Saute beef, onions and garlic in oil until browned; blend in flour. Add tomatoes, tomato paste, herbs, seasonings and water; simmer for 1¼ hours. Add carrots; simmer 1 hour. Combine ziti and cheese; spoon stew over ziti.

Eleanor Skrabal (Mrs. Robert)

Cold Braised Beef Vinaigrette

Serves 4-6

3 T. red wine vinegar
1 t. salt
pepper
1 t. Dijon or dry mustard
9 T. olive oil
2 T. chopped capers
½ t. finely chopped garlic
2 T. chopped parsley
6-8 slices leftover
   cooked beef (¼"
   thick) or 3 c. leftover
   cooked beef, cubed
½ c. thinly sliced onion
chopped parsley
tomato slices
eggs, hard-cooked,
   halved

Combine vinegar, salt, pepper and mustard. Beat in oil. Add capers, garlic and parsley. Place beef in single layer in a shallow dish; top with onions. Pour dressing over all, coating meat thoroughly. Marinate at least 3 hours at room temperature. Sprinkle with additional chopped parsley. Garnish with tomato slices and eggs, drizzled with some of the dressing.

Clara Lorenz

German Beef Rolls-Rouladen

Serves 8

8 slices round steak,
   thinly sliced
mustard
1 lb. bacon, diced,
   crisply cooked
   (reserve drippings)
2 onions, chopped,
   sauteed
bread crumbs
salt and pepper
2-3 pickles, cut
   lengthwise (optional)
flour
2 cans beef bouillon or
   tomato soup, or 1 can
   beef bouillon and 1¼c.
   red wine
spaetzle (German
   noodles) or rice

Spread each beef slice with mustard; sprinkle each with bacon, onion, crumbs, salt and pepper; lay a pickle strip on each, if desired. Roll up; secure with toothpicks. Dredge rolls in flour; brown all sides in bacon drippings. Place in shallow baking dish; pour soup over all. Bake covered at 350° for 1¼-1½ hours, turning occasionally and adding more liquid if necessary. Serve over spaetzle or rice.

Lenore Ford (Mrs. William E., Jr.)
Joan Hyde (Mrs. Arthur)
Bette Shuster (Mrs. Morrison, Jr.)

Bul-Kogi (Korean Barbecue)　　Serves 4

1-1½ lbs. beef flank
　steak, sliced
　diagonally ¼" thick
3 T. sugar
5 T. soy sauce
2 scallions, minced
1 garlic clove, minced
2 t. minced ginger
4 T. rice wine
pepper
3 T. sesame oil
rice
Kimchi (Korean pickles)

Sprinkle beef with sugar ½ hour before cooking. Combine soy sauce, scallions, garlic, ginger, wine and pepper; mix with beef. Stir in sesame oil. Broil or cook over charcoal, using a fine rack. Don't overcook. Serve with rice and Kimchi. (Rice wine and Kimchi can be purchased at Oriental grocery stores.)

Myunghee Reimann

Jab Chai (Korean Chop Suey)　　Serves 6-8

1½ lbs. lean beef, cut in
　thin strips 1½" x ½" x
　½"
1 garlic clove, sliced
3 T. salad oil, divided
1 medium carrot,
　julienned
3 T. sesame oil, divided
2 small onions, sliced
　lengthwise
1 lb. fresh spinach
1 lb. Korean Vermicelli*
2 T. milk
2 eggs
¼ c. soy sauce
1 T. salt
3 T. sugar

*translucent sweet
　potato "spaghetti"

Saute beef and garlic in 2 tablespoons salad oil. Saute carrot strips in 1 tablespoon sesame oil and the remaining salad oil. Saute onions in remaining sesame oil. Wipe the bottom of a large skillet with some salad oil; saute spinach until wilted; cut spinach into strips. Cook vermicelli in unsalted boiling water until clear, tender and swelled to twice its size. Drain; rinse with cold water. Stir milk into eggs. Wipe bottom of small skillet with salad oil; fry egg mixture as for pancakes, ⅓ at a time (will cook through without turning). Cut each of the 3 egg pancakes into strips. Combine all ingredients with soy sauce, salt and sugar. Turn into a 2 quart oven-proof casserole. Heat at 350°, covered, for 30-45 minutes, or turn into a covered crockpot; set on high temperature and heat for 1-1½ hours.

Alice Barstow (Mrs. John)

Quick Chinese Skillet Dinner

Serves 4

1½ lbs. flank steak
½ c. + 2 T. soy sauce
2 garlic cloves, minced
dab ginger and mustard
2 T. sugar, divided
4 T. peanut oil, divided
carrots
scallions
cabbage
spinach
bean sprouts
dash sherry

Marinate steak for 3 hours in ½ cup soy sauce, garlic, ginger, mustard and 1 tablespoon sugar. Freeze for one hour before cooking. Slice meat paper thin; saute quickly in 2 tablespoons oil. Wash pan; add fresh oil. Add any combination of vegetables to hot oil. When tender, return meat to pan. Add remaining soy sauce, sugar and a dash of sherry. Stir; serve over rice.

Joan Hamburg, WOR Radio

Flank Steak Pinwheels

Serves 6-8

2-2½ lbs. flank steak
1 c. oil
⅔ c. water
¼ c. soy sauce
2 t. Worcestershire sauce
1 T. lemon pepper
few drops hot pepper sauce
4 cherry tomatoes
4 mushroom caps

Pound steaks with mallet to tenderize until ¼" thick. Cut into about eight 1½" strips. Combine oil with seasonings. Marinate steak in this mixture for several hours; remove from marinade. Place a tomato on each of four strips and a mushroom on each of 4 strips; roll up and secure each with a skewer. Charcoal-grill or broil for 20-25 minutes, turning to cook evenly. (Note: use the leftover marinade to marinate parboiled potatoes, carrots and small white onions; bake at 350° for 15-20 minutes until tender.)

Gerri Harter (Mrs. William)

Easy Beef Wellington

Serves 6-8

1 4 lb. beef tenderloin
¼ c. dry sherry
¼ t. pepper
1 8 oz. can sliced
   mushrooms, drained
½ t. salt
flour
2 8 oz. pkgs. refrigerated
   crescent rolls
1 egg yolk, beaten

Rub beef with sherry and pepper. Place on rack in shallow pan; bake at 450° for 15 minutes; cool. Puree mushrooms and salt in blender for 1 minute; spread on beef. On lightly floured surface, open rolls, press perforated lines together; roll to 1/8″ thickness. Wrap beef in dough; press together at ends and seam. Any excess may be used to decorate top. Brush with egg yolk. Bake at 350° for 25 minutes.

Adele Merkle (Mrs. Joseph)

Deviled Steak

Serves 6

1½ lbs. sirloin steak, cut
   1″ thick
2 T. butter
1 T. snipped parsley
1 T. dry sherry
1 t. dry mustard
1 t. Worcestershire
   sauce
¼ t. salt
pepper
¼ c. ketchup
1 3 oz. can sliced
   mushrooms, drained

Saute steak to desired doneness in large skillet. Turn off heat; add remaining ingredients, stirring until well combined. Heat until sauce is warm.

David Morrow

Sirloin Steak au Poivre L'Affaire

Serves 4

4 10-12 oz. shell steaks,
   trimmed, or 3½-4 lbs.
   1" thick London Broil
½ c. peppercorns,
   crushed
butter or oil

Sauce:
2 oz. brandy
2 c. heavy cream
salt
2 t. chopped chives

Coat steak on both sides with crushed peppercorns, pressing firmly. Cook steaks in butter or oil over medium heat for 15-20 minutes for medium. Remove steak. Away from flame, add brandy to pan. Carefully return to stove; cook for 2-3 minutes. Add cream, salt, chives and juice from the steak. Reduce over high heat for 3-5 minutes. Pour sauce over steak.

L'Affaire 22, Mountainside

Steak Tartare

Serves 4

2 lbs. lean steak (filet
   mignon or top round),
   very finely ground
4 egg yolks
¼ c. finely chopped
   chives
4 t. finely chopped
   parsley
2 t. paprika
1 t. dry mustard
2 t. Worcestershire
   sauce
dash cayenne pepper
salt
finely ground pepper
2 T. brandy
4 slices rye bread
4 T. capers
4 lemon wedges

In a bowl thoroughly mix chopped steak, egg yolks, chives, seasonings and brandy. Spread mixture on bread slices, garnish with capers and lemon wedges. Serve raw.

Ann Low (Mrs. Calvin)

Blender Bernaise Sauce

Yield: 1 cup

4 egg yolks
1 T. lemon juice
½ t. salt
2 drops Tabasco
1 T. minced onion
2 T. white wine
1 t. tarragon
½ t. chervil
½ c. butter, melted

Put all but butter in blender. Whirl. Gradually add butter with blender on. For hollandaise sauce, omit herbs and wine, using only 3 egg yolks. Can be reheated in a double boiler.

Adele Burnham (Mrs. Bruce)

Herbed Seasoned Topper

Yield: ¾ cup

½ c. butter, softened
2 T. lemon juice
2 T. grated onion
1 t. salt
¼ t. pepper
1 t. ground rosemary
1 t. ground thyme

Whip butter until fluffy; add remaining ingredients. Let stand at room temperature for several hours to blend flavors. Spoon on steaks before removing from grill.

Charlotte Nelson (Mrs. John)

Fluffy Mustard Sauce

Yield: 1⅓ cups

2 egg yolks, beaten
1 T. sugar
3 T. prepared mustard
2 T. vinegar
1 T. water
¾ t. salt
1 T. butter
1 T. prepared
  horseradish
½ c. heavy cream,
  whipped
yellow food coloring

To beaten egg yolks, add sugar, mustard, vinegar, water and salt. Cook over hot, not boiling water, stirring constantly, until mixture thickens, about 4-5 minutes. Remove from heat; blend in butter and horseradish. Adjust color with food coloring. Cool thoroughly. Fold in cream. Store in refrigerator until 30 minutes before serving. Good with beef.

Jean Clutsam (Mrs. Henry O., Jr.)
Jane Stanley (Mrs. Percy)

Poultry

Chicken Angelo

Serves 6

4 whole chicken
   breasts, boned,
   skinned and split
2 eggs, beaten
1 c. Italian bread
   crumbs
4 T. butter, melted
8 oz. fresh mushrooms,
   sliced
¾ lb. Muenster cheese,
   sliced
1½ c. chicken broth

Dip chicken in eggs; coat with bread crumbs. Saute chicken in butter until brown; transfer to 13x9″ baking dish. Sprinkle with half the mushrooms; cover with cheese. Sprinkle with remaining mushrooms; pour broth over all. Bake at 350° for 30-35 minutes.

Anne Lyon (Mrs. Richard)

Blue Ribbon Chicken

Serves 6-8

3 2½ lb. broilers,
   quartered
2 T. butter
salt and pepper
1¼ c. orange juice
½ c. raisins
¼ c. chopped chutney
½ c. blanched almonds,
   split
½ t. cinnamon
1-1½ t. curry powder
sliced bananas
mandarin oranges
optional condiments:
   chopped scallions,
   bacon bits and
   coconut chips

Arrange chicken in a large shallow greased baking dish; dot with butter and sprinkle with salt and pepper. Bake at 425° for 15 minutes until golden brown. Combine orange juice, raisins, chutney, almonds, cinnamon and curry powder; simmer for 10 minutes until flavors blend. Pour sauce over browned chicken; reduce heat to 325° and bake for 1 hour more. Garnish with bananas and oranges. Serve with optional condiments.

Victoria Ott (Mrs. Craig)

Cinnamon-Honey
Barbeque Chicken

Serves 6-8

2 **chickens, 2-2½ lbs.
  each, quartered**
1 **c. dry sherry**
⅔ **c. honey**
4 **t. cinnamon**
2 **t. curry powder**
2 **t. garlic salt**

Arrange chicken in a shallow baking dish. Combine remaining ingredients and pour over chicken. Cover and marinate 2-3 hours at room temperature, or in refrigerator for 8 hours, or overnight. Drain and reserve marinade. Arrange chicken, skin side up, on grill over hot charcoal. Turn every 10 minutes, basting frequently with marinade. Cook slowly for 1 to 1¼ hours until fork-tender.

Gwen Moore (Mrs. David)

Spiced Cherry Chicken

Serves 4

2 **whole chicken
  breasts, split and
  skinned**
salt and pepper
1 **T. oil**
2 **T. butter**
juice of 1 lemon
½ **c. dry red wine**
½ **c. Madeira wine**
¼ **t. ground ginger**
rind of ½ lemon, grated
¼ **c. currant jelly or
  seedless raspberry or
  blackberry preserves**
1 **t. arrowroot or
  cornstarch dissolved
  in 1 T. water**
1½ **c. sour cherries,
  pitted**

Sprinkle chicken with salt and pepper; saute in oil and butter until golden brown; sprinkle with lemon juice. Cover; simmer for 15 minutes until tender. Combine wines, ginger, lemon rind and jelly; heat. Add arrowroot and stir until thickened. Stir in cherries. Arrange chicken on serving platter; spoon cherry sauce over all. Can be made ahead and re-heated.

Ruthelizabeth Lovretin (Mrs. Andrew)

Chicken Chinoise

½ c. soy sauce
¼ c. fresh lemon juice
1 T. chopped fresh coriander
1 t. grated fresh ginger or ½ t. powdered ginger
2 garlic cloves, put through a press
3 whole chicken breasts, boned, skinned and split
1 c. shelled walnuts
¼ c. vegetable oil
1 T. walnut oil
1 c. chicken broth
2 T. cornstarch mixed with ¼ c. water
3 zucchinis
5 carrots
5 stalks celery
1 bunch broccoli
2 scallions, cut in thin strips

Combine soy sauce, lemon juice, coriander, ginger and garlic; marinate chicken in mixture overnight. Next day, saute walnuts for few seconds in the 2 oils combined; drain nuts, reserving oil. Drain chicken, reserving marinade, and saute in reserved oil for 3-5 minutes on each side; remove chicken. Add marinade and broth, bring to a boil and simmer 1 minute. Thicken with cornstarch; pour over chicken and refrigerate until well chilled. Cut vegetables, except scallions, in julienne strips and blanch in boiling water. Slice cold chicken paper-thin and arrange on a platter of lettuce leaves, topping with scallions and walnuts. Surround with vegetables. Serve sauce on side.

Annemarie's Cooking School

"Illegitimate" Cordon Bleu

Serves 4-6

2 c. cooked ham, diced
2 c. chicken, diced (cooked or raw)
¾ lb. aged Swiss cheese
1 can cream of chicken soup
2 T. Worcestershire sauce

Mix all ingredients together in casserole; heat to bubbling at 350° for 30 minutes for cooked chicken; for raw chicken, 1½ hours. Freezes well.

Roland D. Roecker, M.D.

Colonial Williamsburg Chicken

Serves 6

3 whole chicken
   breasts, boned and
   split
4 T. butter, melted
12 fresh mushrooms,
   sauteed
6 thin slices Virginia
   ham

Grape Sauce:
¼ c. butter, melted
¼ c. flour
½ t. salt
2 c. chicken broth
2 T. lemon juice
2 T. sugar
2 c. seedless green
   grapes

Arrange chicken, skin side down, on a foil-lined broiler pan; brush with butter. Broil 3-4″ from heat for 15 minutes. Turn chicken; brush with butter. Lower pan 7-8″ from heat; broil for 15 minutes more or until chicken is cooked. Arrange ham slices in a 13x9″ baking dish; cover each slice with a chicken piece. Pour Grape Sauce over all; top with mushrooms. Bake at 325° for 30 minutes.

Sauce: Blend butter, flour and salt; add chicken broth gradually, stirring constantly until smooth and thick. Mix in lemon juice and sugar; add grapes.

Tiffany Corbett (Mrs. James)

Curried Chicken

Serves 4

2 whole chicken
   breasts, halved,
   skinned, boned
2 T. vegetable oil
2 garlic cloves, minced
2 medium onions,
   chopped
2 c. canned chicken
   broth, boiling
2 T. flour
1-2 T. curry powder
2 t. ground ginger
1 t. salt
2 medium Delicious
   apples, peeled,
   chopped
2 medium tomatoes,
   peeled, chopped

In heavy pot with tight-fitting lid, saute chicken in oil 5 minutes per side. Remove; cut into 1½″ cubes. In same oil, cook garlic and onion 5 minutes until translucent. Stir in flour, curry, ginger and salt. Add boiling chicken broth; stir until smooth. Add apples, tomatoes and chicken. Cover; simmer 20 minutes until apples are soft. Do not overcook. Let stand one hour before serving. Reheat until just bubbly. Serve with rice and chutney.

Morey Wosnitzer, M.D.

Eight-Piece Chicken

Serves 4

1 chicken
1 t. salt
1 clove garlic, minced
1 scallion, cut into 1"
   pieces
2 slices ginger root,
   minced
4 T. soy sauce
2 T. sherry
cornstarch
oil

With a cleaver, chop chicken, bones and all, into eight even pieces. Mix together remaining ingredients except cornstarch and oil. Marinate chicken in this mixture for 2 hours. Drain chicken and dredge lightly in cornstarch. Heat oil. Add chicken, a few pieces at a time, and deep fry until golden.

Victor S. Lamberto, M.D.

Far East Ginger Chicken

Serves 4

½ c. flour
2 t. salt
2 lbs. chicken parts
⅓ c. butter or oil
3 scallions, thinly sliced

Ginger Sauce:
⅛ c. butter
½ c. dry sherry
2 T. soy sauce
2 T. sugar
2 T. lemon juice
2 T. finely chopped
   ginger root

Coat chicken with flour and salt mixture. Saute chicken and scallions lightly in butter. Transfer chicken to a baking dish; pour Ginger Sauce over all. Cover and bake at 350° for 1 hour, turning and basting after 30 minutes. Serve with rice.

Sauce: Combine all ingredients and heat to a boil.

Sally Langenheim (Mrs. Lawson)

Herbed Chicken Rosé

Serves 6

4 whole chicken
   breasts, split
flour
4 T. butter, melted
2 8 oz. cans sliced
   mushrooms or 1 lb.
   fresh mushrooms,
   sliced
½ c. chicken consomme
1½ c. rosé wine
dried tarragon leaves

Dredge chicken in flour; brown in butter. Reserve butter; transfer chicken to a 2 quart baking dish. Brown mushrooms in reserved butter. Add consomme and wine; cook 5 minutes; pour mixture over chicken. Sprinkle top generously with tarragon. Bake, covered, at 350° for 1 hour until chicken is tender.

Judy Faroldo (Mrs. Joseph)

Chicken Piccata

Serves 2

1 whole chicken breast,
  boned and skinned
flour
salt and pepper
1 egg
2-3 T. milk
2 T. butter, melted
1 oz. Chablis wine
juice of ½ lemon
2 T. brown gravy
chopped chives

Cut chicken into 2 parts; pound to flatten. Dredge chicken in flour, salt and pepper. Beat egg and milk together. Dip chicken in egg mixture. Sauté chicken in butter until tender; stir in wine, lemon juice and gravy. Transfer to serving platter; garnish with chives.

Ruth Miller (Mrs. James)

Poulet à la Moutarde

Serves 4-6

4 whole chicken
  breasts, boned,
  skinned and split
salt and pepper
3 T. Dijon mustard
3 T. dry white wine
1 t. Worcestershire
  sauce
2½ c. fresh bread
  crumbs
4 T. butter, melted
4 T. oil

Mustard Cream Sauce:
⅓ c. dry mustard
2 T. water
⅓ c. dry white wine
1 T. white wine vinegar
¼ c. finely chopped
  shallots
1 t. black pepper
1 bay leaf
¼ t. dried thyme
2 c. heavy cream

Pound the chicken to flatten; sprinkle with salt and pepper; brush on all sides with a mixture of the mustard, wine and Worcestershire sauce. Coat firmly with bread crumbs. Saute in butter and oil, cooking for 5-10 minutes on each side until chicken is tender. Serve with Mustard Cream Sauce.

Sauce: Combine mustard and water; let stand 20 minutes. Combine all other ingredients except cream; cook over high heat until liquid is reduced. Stir in cream; cook 10 minutes, stirring often. Add mustard and put through a sieve. Serve hot.

Odille Volpicelli (Mrs. Vincent)

Chicken Parisienne

Serves 4-6

8 boneless chicken
  breast halves, lightly
  sauteed
2 T. butter, melted
1 medium onion,
  minced
2 T. flour
1 c. chicken broth
1 c. white wine
2 t. lemon juice
1 t. sugar
½ t. salt
¼ t. pepper
½ lb. fresh mushrooms,
  sliced

Arrange chicken in a shallow baking dish; set aside. Saute onions lightly in butter; blend in flour until smooth and thickened. Stir in broth and wine; add remaining ingredients. Simmer 3 minutes, stirring constantly. Pour sauce over chicken. Bake at 350° for 25-30 minutes, basting occasionally.

Jane Stanley (Mrs. Percy)

Poulet Piquant

Serves 4-6

3 whole chicken
  breasts, boned and
  split
¾ c. rosé wine
¼ c. soy sauce
¼ c. olive oil
1 garlic clove, sliced
1 t. ground ginger
¼ t. oregano
1 T. brown sugar

Arrange chicken in a baking dish. Combine all other ingredients and pour over chicken. Bake at 325° for 1½ hours.

Simone Moreira (Mrs. Gregory)

Sesame Baked Chicken

Serves 6

2 eggs, slightly beaten
1 T. water
1 T. soy sauce
½ t. salt
¼ t. white pepper
6 whole chicken
  breasts, skinned,
  boned and split
¼ c. flour
½ c. sesame seeds
½ c. melted butter

Combine first five ingredients. Coat chicken with flour; dip into egg mixture and then into sesame seeds. Pour melted butter into shallow baking dish; add chicken, turning to coat. Bake at 375° for 40-50 minutes until golden brown. Serve hot or cold.

Bette Shuster (Mrs. Morrison O., Jr.)

Chicken Scampi

Serves 6-8

8-10 chicken pieces
salt and pepper
¼ c. butter, melted
¼ c. olive oil
3 small onions, sliced
3 T. chopped fresh
   parsley
1 t. basil leaves
1 8 oz. can tomato
   sauce
1 c. red wine
1 lb. raw shrimp, shelled
   and deveined

Sprinkle chicken with salt and pepper; saute in butter and oil until golden. Add onions, parsley, basil, tomato sauce and wine; cover and simmer for 30 minutes until chicken is tender. Add shrimp to one side of pan; increase heat and cook uncovered until shrimp becomes pink and tender. Remove chicken to a serving platter; top with shrimp.

Maryalice Marakas (Mrs. James)

Chicken Sevillana

Serves 8-10

3-3½ lbs. chicken
   breasts, split
3-3½ lbs. chicken legs
   and thighs
olive oil
vegetable oil
3 large onions, chopped
3 large green peppers,
   seeded and chopped
2 T. butter
2 T. olive oil
1½ c. ketchup
1½ c. chicken broth
¾ c. lemon juice
⅓ c. red wine vinegar
⅓ c. brown sugar
3 T. Worcestershire
   sauce
1½ c. dry sherry
¾ c. dry red wine

Brown chicken in combined oils; drain and transfer chicken to heavy roasting pan. Saute onion and pepper in butter and oil until onion is golden. Set aside. Combine ketchup, broth, lemon juice, vinegar, brown sugar and Worcestershire sauce. Stir in onions and peppers; simmer for 20 minutes. Stir in sherry and red wine; pour over chicken. Cover and bake at 350° for 1 hour.

Eileen Helck (Mrs. Jerry)

Chicken Sorrento

6 chicken breast halves,
  boned and skinned
salt and pepper
½ c. butter, melted
¼ lb. mozzarella cheese,
  sliced
½ c. flour
2 eggs, beaten
1 c. Italian bread
  crumbs
1 t. marjoram
½ t. ground thyme
½ c. white wine

Pound chicken to flatten; sprinkle with salt and pepper. Brush butter on top of each piece, reserving unused butter. Cover each piece with a cheese slice. Roll each piece (with cheese on inside) tucking in ends and tying roll with string. Dredge in flour, dip in eggs and roll in bread crumbs. Arrange rolls in baking dish. Baste with a mixture of reserved butter, marjoram and thyme. Bake at 350° for 20 minutes, then add wine. Continue baking for another 20 minutes until tender, basting frequently with pan juices.

Karen Herm

South-of-the-Border Chicken

12 corn tortillas
oil
2 cans cream of chicken
  soup
1 c. chicken broth or
  milk
2 4 oz. cans chopped
  green chilies
3 c. cooked chicken, cut
  in large pieces
1 c. chopped onion
1 c. grated Cheddar
  cheese

Fry the tortillas lightly in hot oil; arrange 6 of them on bottom of a 13x9″ baking dish. Combine soup, broth, chilies and chicken. Layer half this mixture on the tortillas in the baking dish; sprinkle with half the onions and then half of the cheese. Repeat layers beginning with tortillas and ending with cheese. Bake at 350° for 30 minutes.

Janice Stowell (Mrs. Edward)

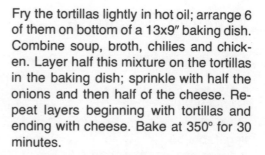

Tarragon Chicken

Serves 3-4

3 whole chicken
   breasts, boned,
   skinned and split
salt and pepper
½ c. dry white wine or
   vermouth
¾ t. tarragon
1 large garlic clove,
   halved
4 T. grated Parmesan
   cheese
paprika

Season chicken with salt and pepper. Marinate for 1 hour at room temperature or overnight in refrigerator in a mixture of wine, tarragon and garlic; stir occasionally. Drain and fold chicken pieces in half lengthwise; arrange in a greased shallow baking dish. Pour marinade over all; sprinkle with cheese and a little paprika. Bake uncovered at 350° for 30-35 minutes until tender. Serve over rice.

Fran Denecke (Mrs. Olin)

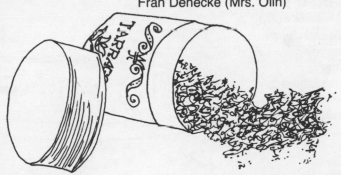

Chicken Stroganoff

Serves 8-10

2½ c. chopped onion
¾ c. butter, divided
1½ c. dry white wine,
   divided
2 lb. mushrooms, sliced
3 T. chopped shallots
3 lbs. chicken breasts,
   boned, skinned, cut in
   1" pieces
1½ c. flour
1 T. salt
¾ t. pepper
⅓ c. ketchup
2 c. sour cream

Saute onions in 4 T. butter until soft; add ¼ c. wine; simmer 5 minutes; set aside. Cook mushrooms in 4 T. butter for 5 minutes; add shallots and cook 3 minutes more. Stir in ½ c. more of the wine and simmer 3 minutes. Remove from heat; combine with onion mixture. Set aside.

Dredge chicken in flour, salt and pepper; brown in remaining butter; transfer chicken to a large flame-proof casserole. Deglaze skillet with balance of wine. Pour pan juices over chicken; stir in onion-mushroom mixture, ketchup and sour cream, mixing well. Heat slowly until hot, but do not boil.

Eileen O'Connor (Mrs. Paul)

Almond Chicken Bake

Serves 6-8

1 6¼ oz. pkg. fast-
   cooking long grain
   and wild rice mix
¼ lb. butter, melted
5-6 whole chicken
   breasts, boned,
   skinned and split
1 can cream of celery
   soup
1 can cream of chicken
   soup
1 can cream of
   mushroom soup
⅛ t. ground thyme
¼ t. pepper
½ c. sherry
½ c. grated sharp
   Cheddar cheese,
   preferably white
½ c. sliced almonds

Pour rice and package seasonings in a 13x9" baking pan; drizzle butter over rice. Roll up each chicken breast and arrange on top of rice. Combine the soups without diluting and spoon over all. Sprinkle with thyme and pepper; pour on sherry. Sprinkle cheese over all; top with almonds. Bake, uncovered, at 275° for 2 hours.

Betty Huson (Mrs. Robert)

Chicken-Rice Bake

Serves 4

1 6¼ oz. pkg. fast-
   cooking long grain
   and wild rice mix or 1
   cup raw rice
1 4 oz. can mushrooms,
   drained
2 T. butter
1½ c. chicken broth
¼ c. sherry
6 boneless chicken
   breast halves
3 T. mayonnaise

Pour rice and package seasonings in a shallow 2½ quart baking dish. Saute mushrooms lightly in butter; add to rice. Pour broth and sherry over all. Arrange chicken on top; brush each piece with 1 t. mayonnaise. Cover and bake at 350° for 30 minutes; uncover and bake at 375° for 20 minutes more until chicken is tender.

Doris Sullivan (Mrs. George)

Chicken and Rice Royale

Serves 8-10

2 3 lb. chickens
1 c. water
1 c. dry sherry
1 onion, sliced
salt
½ t. curry powder
½ c. sliced celery
1 lb. fresh mushrooms
¼ c. butter, melted
2 6¼ oz. pkgs. fast-
    cooking long grain
    and wild rice mix
1 can cream of
    mushroom soup
1 c. sour cream
butter for topping

Simmer chickens for 1 hour in mixture of water, sherry, onion, salt, curry and celery. Remove chicken to cool; strain broth and reserve. De-bone the chicken; set aside. Slice all but 5 or 6 mushrooms; saute sliced and whole mushrooms in butter, reserving whole mushrooms for garnish. Cook rice according to directions for preparing "firm" rice, using reserved broth in liquid amount required. Add chicken and sliced mushrooms. Transfer to a shallow baking dish. Combine soup and sour cream; pour over chicken. Garnish with whole mushrooms; dot with butter. Bake at 350° for 1 hour.

Joan Krikorian (Mrs. John)
Berkeley Hayes (Mrs. William)

Chicken and Sausage Country Style

Serves 25

8 lbs. sausage
10 whole chicken
    breasts, boned,
    skinned
8 lbs. green peppers
1 qt. marinara sauce
4 lbs. onions, cut up
6 4 oz. cans button
    mushrooms, drained
garlic powder
oregano
basil
chopped parsley
salt and pepper
4 14 oz. cans artichoke
    hearts in water,
    drained and rinsed
1½ c. sherry

Cut sausage, chicken and peppers into 1 inch slices. Combine all ingredients except sherry and artichokes; refrigerate overnight. Transfer to a dutch oven and bake at 400° for 45 minutes. Add artichokes and sherry; continue baking for another 30 minutes.

Mary P. Melega (Mrs. Donald)

Soupreme Skillet Chicken

Serves 4

2 lbs. cut-up chicken
paprika
2 T. shortening
1 can cream of celery
soup
1 t. basil leaves
¼ t. instant minced
garlic
1 16 oz. can tomatoes,
drained and chopped
2 medium zucchini, cut
lengthwise and sliced
into ½" pieces

Sprinkle chicken with paprika; brown in shortening; pour off fat. Add soup, basil and garlic; cover and cook slowly for 30 minutes, stirring occasionally. Add tomatoes and zucchini; continue cooking, covered, for another 30 minutes until zucchini is tender. Serve over rice.

Peggy Trentin (Mrs. H. George)

Chicken Stew Italiano

Serves 6-8

2 T. oil
½ lb. sweet Italian
sausage, cut into 1"
pieces
3½ lbs. chicken, cut up
6 c. celery, cut into 2"
pieces
½ c. minced onion
1 1 lb. can stewed
tomatoes
salt
½ t. oregano
2 c. potatoes, cut into 1"
cubes or 8 small red
potatoes
1 T. flour
1 T. cold water

Heat oil in Dutch oven; add sausage; brown for 5 minutes. Remove sausage; set aside. Brown chicken on all sides. Remove; set aside. Saute celery and onions for 5 minutes. Return sausage and chicken to the pan along with tomatoes, salt and oregano. Bring to boil; cover; simmer for 15 minutes. Add potatoes; simmer for 30 minutes until chicken and potatoes are done. Blend flour with water, stir into sauce. Cook for 5 minutes until sauce is slightly thickened.

Marian Stuart (Mrs. Russell)

Swiss Chicken-Ham Bake

Serves 6

½ c. chopped onion
2 T. butter
3 T. flour
½ t. salt
¼ t. pepper
1 3 oz. can sliced
  mushrooms
1 c. light cream
2 T. dry sherry
2 c. cubed, cooked
  chicken or turkey
1 c. cubed cooked ham
1 5 oz. can water
  chestnuts, drained
  and sliced
1 c. grated Swiss
  cheese
¾ c. bread crumbs
3 T. butter, melted

Saute onion in butter until soft. Blend in flour, salt and pepper. Add undrained mushrooms, cream and sherry; cook until thickened. Fold in chicken, ham and water chestnuts. Pour into 1½ quart greased baking dish. Top with cheese and crumbs. Drizzle butter over top. Bake at 400° for 20 minutes until brown and bubbly.

Dode Macy (Mrs. Theodore)
Julie Ann Planck (Mrs. J. Kent)

Chicken Breasts Wellington

Serves 16

8 whole chicken
  breasts, boned,
  skinned and split
16 Pepperidge Farm
  frozen patty shells,
  thawed
Dijon mustard
16 slices Swiss cheese
16 slices cooked ham

Mushroom Sauce:
2 cans cream of
  mushroom soup
1 pt. sour cream

Poach chicken in lightly salted water for 30 minutes; drain and cool slightly. Meanwhile, roll out each patty shell into a 6″ square. Spread mustard on each square; top each with one piece of chicken wrapped in a slice of cheese and a slice of ham. Wrap the patty shell around the chicken-ham-cheese combination; place on baking sheet and bake at 400° for 30-40 minutes. Serve with mushroom sauce.

Sauce: Mix soup and sour cream. Heat thoroughly and serve.

Mary Kay Reber (Mrs. George)

Chicken Pasties

2 3 oz. pkgs. cream
   cheese, softened
2 T. butter
2 c. diced cooked
   chicken
¼ t. salt
⅛ t. pepper
2 T. milk
1 T. chopped onion
1 T. chopped pimiento
   (optional)
2 8 oz. cans refrigerated
   crescent dinner rolls
melted butter
1 T. bread crumbs

Mushroom Sauce:
1 can cream of
   mushroom soup
¼ c. milk or chicken
   broth
1 c. sour cream
¼ c. chopped pimientos

Blend cream cheese with butter; add chicken, salt, pepper, milk, onion and, if desired, pimiento. Set aside. Separate the rolls into rectangles; arrange on ungreased baking sheet. Cover each rectangle with chicken mixture; pinch all 4 corners together. Brush top of each with butter; sprinkle with bread crumbs. Bake at 350° for 20-25 minutes. Serve with Mushroom Sauce.

Sauce: Mix all ingredients until well blended. Heat thoroughly.

Cathe Dalecki (Mrs. Robert)

Hot Chicken Salad

4 c. diced cooked
   chicken
2 c. chopped celery
2 T. lemon juice
¾ c. mayonnaise
4 hard-cooked eggs,
   sliced
¾ c. cream of chicken
   soup
2 pimientos, finely cut
1 t. finely minced onion

Topping:
1½ c. crushed potato
   chips
1 c. grated Cheddar
   cheese
⅔ c. sliced toasted
   almonds

Combine all ingredients except topping in a casserole dish. Cover with topping and bake at 400° for 20-25 minutes.

Eleanor Skrabal (Mrs. Robert)
Kekee Szorcsik (Mrs. J. Mitchell)

Mother's Best Chicken Salad

Serves 12

6 whole chicken breasts
1 qt. chicken stock
few sprigs parsley
1 onion, quartered
2 stalks celery
6 stalks celery, finely
  chopped
1 dill pickle, finely
  chopped
1 3½ oz. jar capers,
  undrained
¼ c. salad oil
½ c. cider vinegar
mayonnaise
lettuce
olives, black and green
deviled eggs
cherry tomatoes

Poach chicken until tender in stock with parsley, onion and 2 stalks of the celery. Cool and de-bone chicken; combine chicken with remaining celery and pickle. Add undrained capers. Combine oil and vinegar; pour over chicken mixture. Refrigerate for a few hours or overnight. Drain chicken; add mayonnaise to taste. Serve in lettuce cups garnished with olives, deviled eggs and cherry tomatoes.

Angela Davis (Mrs. Thomas)

Cornish Game Hens

Serves 6

6 Cornish Game hens
  (1¼ lbs. each)
7 T. tarragon, divided
salt and pepper
6 garlic cloves
garlic salt
butter
¾ c. dry white wine
2 T. flour
1 c. water
wild rice

Wash and dry hens. Sprinkle inside each with ¼ teaspoon salt, ⅛ teaspoon pepper and 1 tablespoon tarragon. Place a garlic clove in each hen. Sprinkle outside liberally with garlic salt. Tie up legs. Baste with melted butter combined with wine and remaining tarragon. Bake in shallow pan at 450° for 1 hour, basting often. Remove from pan; keep warm. Dissolve flour in water; stir into pan drippings. Bring to a boil, stirring until thickened. Mound wild rice in center of platter; surround with hens.

Calvin D. Low

Turkey Divan

2   10 oz. pkgs. frozen
    broccoli spears
    or 2 9 oz. pkgs. frozen
    cut green beans
4   c. cooked, cut up
    turkey or chicken
2   cans cream of chicken
    soup
1   c. mayonnaise
1   t. lemon juice
½ t. curry powder
1   c. sliced water
    chestnuts (optional)
½ c. grated American
    cheese
½ c. bread crumbs
1   T. butter, melted

Cook vegetables until barely tender; drain and arrange in a greased baking dish; place turkey on top. Combine soup, mayonnaise, lemon juice, curry, and, if desired, water chestnuts; pour over turkey or chicken. Sprinkle with cheese. Combine bread crumbs and butter and sprinkle over all. Bake at 350° for 25-30 minutes.

Lillian Buehrer (Mrs. Arthur)
Barbara Gill (Mrs. Robert)

Goodbye Turkey

⅓ c. flour
1   t. salt, divided
¼ t. onion salt
¼ c. butter
2½ c. milk
1½ c. fast cooking rice
1½ c. turkey or chicken
    broth
½ c. grated Cheddar
    cheese
1½ c. cooked asparagus
    spears
6   large slices cooked
    turkey (or 2 c. cut-up)
1   c. cubed cooked ham
2   T. toasted slivered
    almonds

Make a cream sauce of the first five ingredients, using half the salt. Pour rice in a shallow 2 quart baking dish. Combine broth and remaining salt; pour over rice. Sprinkle half the cheese on top. Lay asparagus spears, turkey and ham on top. Pour cream sauce over all. Sprinkle with remaining cheese and almonds. Bake at 375° for 20-30 minutes until bubbly.

Peggy Trentin (Mrs. H. George)

Florentine Fantasy

1 12 lb. turkey breast
2 t. salt
¼ c. peppercorns
4 carrots
6 stalks celery
3 lbs. fresh spinach
½ lb. plus 2 T. butter
salt and pepper
¼ t. nutmeg
½ c. flour
8 c. turkey broth
2 c. heavy cream
16 oz. kluski noodles
2 egg yolks, lightly
    beaten
1 c. grated Parmesan
    cheese

Place turkey in a large kettle; cover with cold water; add salt, peppercorns, carrots and celery. Bring to a boil and simmer for 2 hours until turkey is cooked and tender. Reserve broth. Cool and de-bone meat; cut into bite-size pieces and set aside. Cook spinach briefly until leaves begin to wilt. Drain and toss with 2 tablespoons butter. Season with salt, pepper and nutmeg. Set aside. Melt half the remaining butter; blend in flour; add broth and cook sauce 45 minutes, stirring frequently. Stir in cream; cook 10 minutes.

Cook noodles until al dente. Drain. In 2 large baking dishes arrange noodles, spinach, and turkey in layers. Pour half the sauce over layers and gently stir in, keeping layers neat. Combine egg yolks with remaining sauce; pour over layers. Sprinkle with cheese; dot with remaining butter. Bake at 400° until heated thoroughly. Brown for a few minutes under broiler.

Maryalice Marakas (Mrs. James)

Pork,
Lamb, Veal

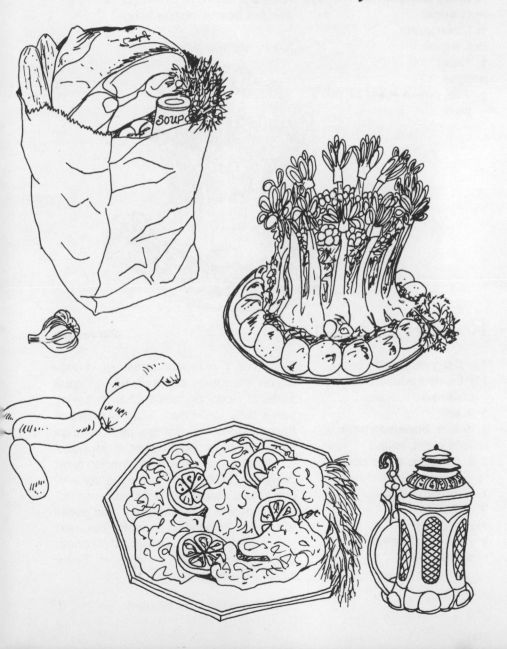

Crown Roast with Cranberries

Serves 6

4 c. bread cubes
2 T. grated onion
1 garlic clove, minced
½ c. butter
**1½ c. chopped raw
    cranberries**
½ c. dry white wine
¼ c. sugar
½ t. marjoram
½ t. thyme
1 t. salt
pepper
**1 7 lb. crown roast of
    pork**

Saute bread, onion and garlic in butter for 10 minutes; add cranberries, wine, sugar and seasonings; spoon into center of roast. Cover the tips of the roast with foil to prevent burning. Roast at 325° for 3½ hours or until meat thermometer registers 185°. Remove coverings from tips 15 minutes before meat is done.

Nancy Morrow (Mrs. David)

Roast Pork à l'Orange

Serves 6-8

1⅛ t. dry mustard
**1⅛ t. dried marjoram,
    crushed**
1 t. salt
**1 5-6 lb. boneless pork
    loin roast, rolled**
2 t. grated orange peel
½ c. orange juice
1 T. brown sugar
3 T. flour
1½ c. water
**2 oranges, peeled,
    sectioned**

Combine 1 teaspoon mustard, 1 teaspoon marjoram and salt; rub on meat surface. Roast on rack in shallow baking pan at 325° for 3 hours. Skim fat from pan juices. Combine orange peel, orange juice and sugar; spoon over meat. Roast for 30 minutes until meat thermometer registers 170°, basting frequently with pan juices. Remove roast to serving platter. Combine 3 tablespoons pan juices with flour, remaining mustard and marjoram. Add water, stir until thickened. Correct seasoning; stir in oranges. Serve sauce with pork.

Alice Stonaker (Mrs. Robert)

Pork and Potatoes

Serves 6

2 lbs. potatoes, thinly
   sliced
½ onion, chopped
½ c. chopped parsley,
   divided
salt and pepper
1 10½ oz. can
   consomme
1 4 lb. boneless rolled
   pork roast
2 T. flour
garlic powder
basil

Layer potatoes in shallow baking dish. Sprinkle with onion, ¼ cup of the parsley, salt and pepper; add consomme. Coat roast with combined flour, garlic powder, basil, remaining parsley, additional salt and pepper. Place on top of potatoes. Roast at 350° for 2 hours.

Lonnie McKown (Mrs. James, III)

Tenderloin with Mustard Sauce

Serves 4

1 3 lb. fresh pork
   tenderloin
¼ c. soy sauce
¼ c. bourbon
2 T. brown sugar
⅓ c. sour cream
⅓ c. mayonnaise
1 T. dry mustard
1 T. chopped green
   onions
1½ t. vinegar
salt

Marinate pork tenderloin in combined soy sauce, bourbon and brown sugar for several hours at room temperature. Remove from marinade; roast at 325° for 1½-2 hours, basting with marinade. Slice; serve with sauce of combined sour cream, mayonnaise, mustard, onions, vinegar and salt.

Bobbie Tooher (Mrs. James)

Chinese Oven-Fried Pork Chops

Serves 4

1 egg
3 T. soy sauce
1 T. dry sherry
⅛ t. ground ginger
½ t. garlic powder
4 T. bread crumbs
4 lean loin pork chops,
   ½" thick, trimmed

Combine egg, soy sauce, sherry, ginger and garlic powder. Dip chops into egg mixture; coat with crumbs; place in single layer in greased baking dish. Bake at 350° for 30 minutes. Turn, bake an additional 20 minutes until tender.

Dorris Irving (Mrs. Stephen)

Pork Chop and Stuffing Loaf

Serves 4

4 ½" thick pork chops,
  trimmed
salt and pepper
1½ c. herb-seasoned
  stuffing mix
1 t. poultry seasoning
¾ c. chopped unpared
  apples
¼ c. seedless raisins
¼ c. chopped celery
¼ c. chopped onion

Season pork chops with salt and pepper. Prepare stuffing mix according to package directions; toss with remaining ingredients. In center of a 2-foot length of foil, stand chops on end, bone side down; run a skewer through centers of chops, spacing them ½" apart. Spoon stuffing between chops. Enclose chops with foil, sealing securely. Bake at 450° for 1¼ hours.

Helen Rossmeisl (Mrs. Herbert J., Jr.)

Pork Chops in Wine Plum Sauce

Serves 4

4 thick loin pork chops,
  trimmed
salt and pepper
sage
flour
1 small jar baby food
  strained plums
½ c. tawny port wine
1 t. grated lemon peel
½ t. cinnamon
¼ t. ground cloves

Season pork chops with salt, pepper and sage; dredge in flour; lightly brown on both sides. Combine remaining ingredients; pour over chops in a greased shallow baking dish. Bake, covered, at 325° for 50 minutes. Add small amount of water if necessary to prevent sauce from drying out.

Elizabeth Miebach

Chinese Barbecued Spareribs

Serves 2-4

¼ c. chicken stock
1 t. brown bean sauce,
   mashed into a paste
   (optional)
4 garlic cloves, minced
4 T. dark Chinese soy
   sauce
4 T. honey
3 T. hoisin sauce
1 T. sherry
1 sheet spareribs
   (12-14 ribs)

Heat chicken stock; mix in remaining ingredients except ribs. Marinate whole sheet of ribs in chicken stock mixture at least 6 hours. Bake ribs with marinade at 375° for 15 minutes. Lower oven to 300°; bake an additional 10 minutes. At this point the ribs may be cooled and refrigerated until needed. Before serving, cut ribs into individual portions, place on rack; broil for 5-10 minutes until brown and crisp on all sides.

Diane Lebovitz (Mrs. Peter)

East Indian Spareribs Sauce

spareribs
1 T. curry powder
1 8 oz. can crushed
   pineapple
¼ c. water
1 t. salt
¼ c. chopped scallions
¼ t. ginger
⅛ c. lemon juice
¼ c. sherry

While ribs are baking at 350° for 30 minutes, combine sauce ingredients except sherry. Boil 2 minutes; add sherry. Spoon over ribs. Bake 1 hour longer.

Howard Baldwin

Ham and Noodle Casserole

Serves 4-6

1 small onion, finely
   chopped
4 T. butter
2 eggs, slightly beaten
1 c. sour cream
½ c. grated Gruyere or
   Swiss cheese
1½ c. finely chopped
   cooked ham
salt
8 oz. ¼" noodles, cooked

Cook onion in butter until soft. Mix eggs with sour cream; add onion, cheese, ham and salt. Put noodles into buttered 2 quart casserole. Add sauce; toss gently. Bake at 350° for 45 minutes until a knife inserted in middle comes out clean.

Leanna Brown (Mrs. Stanley)

Ham and Asparagus Casserole   Serves 6

1 10 oz. pkg. frozen cut
   asparagus, cooked
2 c. diced cooked ham
¼ c. grated Cheddar
   cheese
2 T. tapioca
2 T. chopped green
   pepper
2 T. chopped onion
1 T. chopped parsley
1 T. lemon juice
2 eggs, hard-cooked,
   sliced
1 can cream of
   mushroom soup
½ c. milk
2 T. butter, melted
½ c. bread crumbs

Place asparagus in a greased 1½ quart baking dish. Combine ham, cheese, tapioca, green pepper, onion, parsley and lemon juice; spread ½ of mixture over asparagus. Lay eggs on top; spread with remaining ham mixture. Combine soup and milk; pour over all. Sprinkle with combined butter and crumbs. Bake at 375° for 25-30 minutes.

Jean Dodson (Mrs. Thomas)

Zucchini-Ham-Cheese Pie   Serves 6

1 large onion, thinly
   sliced
3 small zucchini, thinly
   sliced
1 garlic clove, crushed
⅓ c. oil
2 c. slivered cooked
   ham
1 c. Swiss cheese,
   shredded
1¼ c. sour cream
1 t. dillweed
salt and pepper
1 9" or 10" deep pie
   shell, baked
2 T. butter, melted
½ c. bread crumbs
¼ c. Parmesan cheese

Saute onion, zucchini and garlic in oil for 5 minutes until zucchini is tender but crisp. Mix in ham, Swiss cheese, sour cream, dillweed, salt and pepper; spoon into pie shell. Combine butter, crumbs and Parmesan cheese; sprinkle over pie. Bake at 350° for 35 minutes until bubbly. Let stand 10 minutes before cutting.

Charlotte Forristel (Mrs. Harry)

Baked Frankfurters and Limas

Serves 14

1 lb. pkg. dried Lima beans, soaked
8 slices bacon, cut into 2″ pieces
¾ c. sliced celery
¾ c. coarsley chopped onion
¼ c. diced green pepper
1 garlic clove, minced
4 T. flour
3 T. sugar
1 t. salt
¼ t. pepper
garlic powder
2 c. canned tomatoes
5 frankfurters, sliced

Cook beans in water to cover until tender. Cook bacon until lightly browned; add celery, onion, green pepper and garlic; cook until tender. Drain, reserving 4 tablespoons of the fat. Make paste of flour and reserved fat; stir in sugar, salt, pepper and garlic powder. Combine beans, bacon mixture, tomatoes and frankfurters in bean pot or casserole. Bake at 300° for 1 hour.

Eleanor Skrabal (Mrs. Robert)

Italian Sweet Sausage with Beans

Serves 4

1 lb. Italian sweet sausage
1 medium onion, chopped
½ c. chopped green pepper
1 garlic clove, crushed
¼ c. dry white wine
1 20 oz. can white cannellini beans, drained, rinsed
1 bay leaf
½ t. salt
¼ t. pepper
2 small tomatoes, chopped

Steam sausage in ¼″ water until liquid evaporates, turning occasionally. Push to one side. Saute onion, green pepper and garlic until tender; stir in wine. Combine all ingredients; simmer covered for 15 minutes.

Elsie Roller (Mrs. Joseph)

Fettuccini La Scala

4-6 servings

¾ lb. sweet Italian
   sausage, casing
   removed
¾ lb. mushrooms, cut in
   ½" slices
½ c. plus 2 T. butter
½ pt. heavy cream
1 egg yolk
1 c. Parmesan cheese,
   divided
pinch of nutmeg
1 12 oz. box fettuccini
   noodles, cooked,
   drained

Brown sausage until well cooked; drain. Saute mushrooms in 2 T. butter until transparent; set aside. Combine remaining butter, cream, egg, ¾ cup cheese and nutmeg; simmer until cheese melts and sauce is smooth. Combine sausage, mushrooms and sauce with hot noodles; toss together and serve. Garnish with remaining cheese. Can be prepared ahead; postpone cooking noodles until ready to serve.

Kathleen Diaz (Mrs. Israel)

Roast Lamb with Herb Sauce

Serves 6-7

4½ c. dry white wine
2 small onions, peeled,
   stuck with cloves
2 garlic cloves, crushed
12 peppercorns
12 juniper berries
2 t. salt
2 carrots, quartered
4 parsley sprigs
2 bay leaves
2 mint sprigs or 1 t.
   dried mint
1 t. thyme
1 6½-7 lb. leg of lamb
¼ c. oil
pepper
2 T. finely chopped
   shallots
3 T. butter
1 c. canned beef gravy
½ c. beef broth, bouillon
   or consomme
¼ c. chopped parsley

Combine wine, onions, garlic, peppercorns, berries, salt, carrots, parsley, bay leaves, mint and ½ of the thyme; pour over lamb; marinate in refrigerator for two days, turning occasionally. Remove lamb from marinade, reserving marinade. Dry well; rub with oil; sprinkle with additional salt and pepper. Roast on rack in roasting pan at 450° for 15 minutes; reduce to 350°; continue to roast for 15 minutes per pound until done, turning lamb occasionally. Strain marinade into saucepan; cook over high heat until almost reduced by half. Saute shallots in butter until golden; add 1 cup of the marinade and remaining ingredients; simmer for 5-10 minutes; serve sauce with lamb.

Nancy Morrow (Mrs. David)

Gingered Butterfly Lamb

Serves 8

⅛ c. peeled minced
 ginger root
½ c. olive oil
½ c. lime juice
¼ c. minced onion
1½ T. grenadine
½ t. ground coriander
2 garlic cloves, minced
1 t. salt
¼ t. ground cumin
¼ t. pepper
cayenne
1 7 lb. boned,
 butterflied leg of
 lamb, pounded to
 even thickness
watercress
kumquats

Alternate marinade:
½ c. oil
½ c. bourbon
½ c. lemon juice
1 t. rosemary
1 t. salt
1 onion, chopped
⅛ t. pepper

Combine first 11 ingredients in blender for 2 minutes; pour over lamb. Marinate at least 8 hours in refrigerator, covered, basting occasionally. Remove from marinade, pat dry; cook over charcoal or broil 3″ from heat for 10-15 minutes on each side. Let stand for 10 minutes before diagonally slicing ½″ thick. Garnish with watercress and kumquats.

Mary Kay Reber (Mrs. George)
Alice Stonaker (Mrs. Robert)

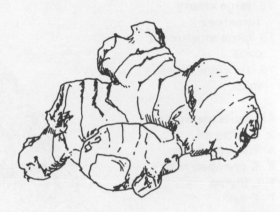

Lamb with Artichoke Stuffing

Serves 4-6

1 2½-3½ lb. boned leg
 of lamb
1 garlic clove
salt and pepper
⅓ c. chopped onion
3 T. butter
1 14 oz. can artichoke
 hearts, drained,
 chopped
1 c. Italian bread
 crumbs
1 T. chopped dill
1 can consomme

Rub lamb inside and out with garlic; sprinkle with salt and pepper. Saute onion in butter; add artichokes. Cook 1 minute; mix in crumbs and dill. Spread mixture inside lamb; secure with skewers. Bake on rack in roasting pan at 325° for 35 minutes per pound; baste with consomme 20 minutes before done. Use pan drippings for gravy, if desired.

Joanne Keith (Mrs. James)

Lamb Shish Kabobs

4 T. lemon juice
5 T. olive oil
2 T. chopped onion
1 t. coriander seeds
1 t. ginger
1 garlic clove, chopped
2 t. turmeric or curry powder
3 t. salt
3 lbs. lean lamb, cut into 1-1½" cubes
12 small white onions, parboiled
18 large cherry tomatoes
18 large mushroom caps
18 zucchini slices, 1" thick

Alternate marinade:
½ c. olive oil
4 T. lemon juice
2 T. chopped mint
1 t. thyme
1 T. salt
pepper

Combine first 8 ingredients; add lamb; marinate at least 4 hours, stirring occasionally. Thread lamb on 6 kebob swords alternately with vegetables. Cook over charcoal or broil 4" from heat until done, turning frequently and basting with marinade.

Sue Eldon (Mrs. David)
Pat Guinivan (Mrs. Thomas)
Jo Powers (Mrs. Mark)

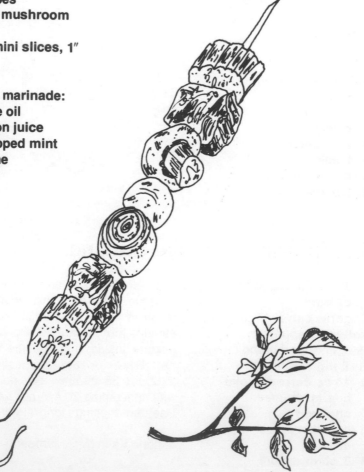

Lamb Shanks in Wine Sauce

Serves 4

1 large onion, chopped
2 T. olive oil
4 lamb shanks
1 garlic clove, minced
3 T. vinegar
3 T. lemon juice
2 T. brown sugar
⅓ c. ketchup
½ c. dry red wine
½ t. salt
⅛ t. pepper
1 t. rosemary, crushed

Saute onion in oil until tender but not brown; remove onion. Brown lamb shanks in same oil; add remaining ingredients. Simmer covered for 3 hours until tender. Serve with noodles or rice.

Mary Elizabeth Kemmerer (Mrs. John)

Lamb 'n Limas

Serves 8-10

1 lb. dried lima beans
6 c. water
2 lbs. onions, sliced
⅛ + ¼ t. garlic powder
¼ c. butter, melted
1 35 oz. can Italian plum
   tomatoes, drained
1 t. dried rosemary
1 t. dried thyme
3 t. salt
1 8-10 lb. leg of lamb
½ t. tarragon
chopped parsley

Combine beans and water; simmer for 2 minutes; let stand covered for 1 hour. Drain, reserving liquid. Add additional water to reserved liquid to measure 2 quarts. Return beans to liquid; simmer covered for 1 hour until tender. Saute onions and ⅛ teaspoon of the garlic powder in butter until golden. In shallow roasting pan combine onions, beans, tomatoes, ½ teaspoon rosemary, ½ teaspoon thyme and 2 teaspoons salt. Sprinkle lamb with remaining rosemary, thyme, garlic powder, salt and tarragon; lay on top of bean mixture. Roast uncovered for 3-3½ hours. Garnish with parsley.

Sharon Remlinger (Mrs. Donald)

Veal with Artichoke Hearts

Serves 6

1½ lb. veal scallops
½ c. flour
1 t. salt
pepper
½ c. milk
½ c. bread crumbs
3 T. oil
1   14 oz. can artichoke
    hearts, drained
2   tomatoes, peeled,
    seeded, cut into
    eighths
2-3   T. consomme or dry
    white wine
Parmesan cheese

Dredge veal in seasoned flour; dip in milk, then coat with crumbs; chill 1 hour. Saute lightly in oil for 5 minutes; transfer to a shallow ovenproof dish. In same skillet heat artichoke hearts and tomatoes, adding wine or consommé to dissolve brown particles. Add to veal; sprinkle with cheese. Bake covered at 350° for 20 minutes.

Marjorie Paul (Mrs. Donald)

Lemon Veal

Serves 4

1   lb. veal scallopini
¾ c. flour
2   T. oil
6   T. butter, divided
salt and pepper
3   T. lemon juice
2   T. minced parsley
1   T. minced basil
1   lemon, thinly sliced

Pound veal; coat with flour. Saute in combined oil and 2 tablespoons of butter until lightly browned. Season with salt and pepper. Remove from pan. Add lemon juice to pan with remaining butter, parsley and basil. Return veal to pan to warm. Garnish with lemon slices.

Susan Johnson (Mrs. Roger)

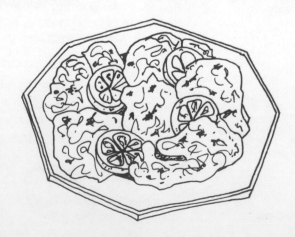

Broiled Veal Scallops

Serves 8

3-4 lbs. veal scallops,
   lightly sauteed
lemon juice
1 c. sour cream
1 c. grated Swiss
   cheese

Lightly saute veal; sprinkle with lemon juice. Let stand 10 minutes. Cover with sour cream; refrigerate overnight. Sprinkle with cheese; broil until browned.

Betty Gorman (Mrs. Paul)

Veal Paprikash

Serves 2

⅔ lb. boneless veal,
   cubed
2 T. fat
1 medium onion, sliced
2 bouillon cubes,
   dissolved in 1 c. water
½ t. salt
½ t. paprika
1 T. flour
½ c. sour cream

Brown veal in fat slowly. Add onion until lightly browned. Add bouillon, salt, and paprika. Cover and cook over low heat for 1 hour until meat is tender. Add more water as needed. Blend flour with 2 tablespoons water. Stir into the meat mixture; cook until thickened. Just before serving, add sour cream. Heat and serve with dumplings or noodles.

Lynn Ferentchak (Mrs. Rudy)

Baked Veal Chops with Cheese

Serves 6

6 loin veal chops, 1"
   thick
½ c. butter
1 bouillon cube
½ c. water
4 T. sherry
salt and pepper
½ lb. Swiss cheese,
   thinly sliced

Brown chops in butter. Dissolve bouillon cube in water; add sherry. Pour over chops, singly layered in shallow baking dish. Sprinkle with salt and pepper; top with cheese. Bake at 350° for 35 minutes.

Charlanne Lamberto (Mrs. Victor)

Zaviany Bytky (Veal Rolls)

Serves 8

¼ lb. ground beef
¼ lb. ground lean pork
2 T. bread crumbs
¼ c. cream
1 egg
1½ t. salt
¼ t. pepper
1 T. minced onion
3 T. chopped parsley
8 veal cutlets, 5x2½x½"
3 T. butter, melted
1 14 oz. can sliced
   mushrooms,
   undrained
½ pt. sour cream
1 t. sugar

Combine first 9 ingredients; spoon 2 heaping tablespoons of mixture on one end of each veal cutlet; roll, beginning at filled end; secure with skewers; brown in butter. Add mushrooms and sour cream; simmer covered for 45 minutes until tender. Season sauce with sugar and additional salt and pepper.

LaVerne Bajorek (Mrs. Robert)

Veal and Pork Casserole

Serves 6-8

1 lb. lean veal, cubed
1 lb. lean pork, cubed
3 T. butter
2 c. water
salt and pepper
2 medium onions,
   chopped
1 small green pepper,
   chopped
1 c. cream of mushroom
   soup
½ lb. Cheddar cheese,
   cubed
1 4 oz. jar pimientos,
   chopped
½ lb. thin noodles,
   cooked
1 c. sour cream

Brown meat in butter; add water, salt and pepper. Bake, covered, at 350° for 1 hour until tender; drain, reserving pan juices. Combine juices with onions, green pepper, soup, cheese, pimientos and noodles. Add to meat; spread with sour cream. Bake at 325° for 2 hours.

Anne Quakenbush (Mrs. J.E.)

Veal Marengo

2 lbs. veal shoulder, cubed
2 T. vegetable oil
2 T. olive oil
salt and pepper
2 T. flour
2 T. tomato paste
1 garlic clove, mashed
1 c. dry white wine
1 10¾ oz. can chicken broth
1 bouquet garni (2 sprigs parsley, 1 bay leaf, 1 celery top)
1 t. thyme
20 small frozen whole onions
2 T. butter
1 c. mushrooms
1 tomato, peeled, cut into eighths
3 t. chopped parsley

Brown veal in oils; sprinkle with salt, pepper, and flour; saute, stirring, for 2-3 minutes. Add tomato paste, garlic, wine, broth, bouquet garni and thyme; simmer for 1 hour. Saute onions in butter until lightly browned; add mushrooms, continue to saute until browned, adding more butter if necessary. Add onions and mushrooms to veal; simmer for 20 minutes. Add tomato; simmer for 10 minutes. Garnish with parsley.

Joan Stettler (Mrs. Wayne)

Seafood

Crabmeat Casserole

Serves 8-12

2 6 oz. pkgs. frozen
  crabmeat, flaked
1 14 oz. can artichoke
  hearts, drained,
  quartered
6 eggs, hard-cooked,
  chopped coarsely
2 c. half and half cream
2 c. Hellmann's
  mayonnaise
3 c. diced white bread
2 T. dried parsley
1 small onion, chopped
2 t. salt
bread crumbs

Combine all ingredients; pour into lightly greased 3 quart casserole or 9x13" pyrex baking dish. Top with bread crumbs; bake at 350° for 30 minutes. Can be prepared a day ahead.

The Committee

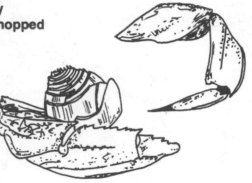

Crab Souffle

Serves 8

8 slices white bread
2 c. crabmeat
½ c. mayonnaise
1 medium onion,
  chopped
1 c. chopped celery
¼ c. chopped green
  pepper
2 c. coarsely shredded
  Cheddar cheese,
  divided
4 eggs, beaten
3 c. milk
1 can cream of
  mushroom soup
paprika

Cube 4 of the bread slices; arrange in bottom of a greased deep 2 quart baking dish. Combine crabmeat, mayonnaise, onion, celery, green pepper and half of the cheese; spoon over bread cubes. Trim crusts from remaining bread slices; arrange over crabmeat mixture. Combine eggs and milk; pour over bread. Chill, covered, at least 8 hours. Bake at 325° uncovered for 15 minutes. Spread soup over bread slices; top with remaining cheese. Sprinkle with paprika; bake 1 hour.

Diane Bourisseau (Mrs. Dale)
Viola Heerwagen (Mrs. Howard)

Scallop Salad

Serves 3-4

1 c. water
½ c. dry white wine
½ t. salt
½ bay leaf
1 scallion, sliced
1 lb. scallops
½ lb. mushrooms, sliced
⅓ c. wine vinegar
¼ c. oil
2 T. chopped parsley
¼ t. pepper
1 medium head iceberg
   lettuce
2-3 eggs, hard-cooked,
   quartered

Combine water, wine, salt, bay leaf and scallion; simmer 5 minutes. Add scallops and mushrooms; simmer, covered, 5 minutes until tender. Drain scallops and mushrooms; mix with vinegar, oil, parsley and pepper. Chill. Line salad bowl or plates with lettuce leaves; cut remaining lettuce into 1" pieces; toss with scallop mixture. Garnish with eggs.

Carolyn Walters

Shrimp and Artichoke Casserole

Serves 6

4½ T. butter
2-2½ T. flour
2 5⅓ oz. cans
   evaporated milk or
   1¼ c. cream
salt and pepper
1 14 oz. can artichoke
   hearts, drained, halved
   or quartered
1 6 oz. jar marinated
   artichoke hearts,
   drained
2 lbs. shrimp, cooked
1 lb. fresh mushrooms,
   sauteed
¼ c. dry sherry
1 T. Worcestershire
   sauce
1 dash Tabasco sauce
Parmesan cheese
paprika

Make a white sauce of butter, flour, milk, salt and pepper. Combine with remaining ingredients, except cheese and paprika. Turn into a baking dish; sprinkle with cheese and paprika. Bake at 350° for 20-30 minutes until bubbly.

Mabel Ehlert (Mrs. William)

Cheesy Shrimp with Asparagus

Serves 6

2 lbs. fresh asparagus, trimmed
1 can cream of celery soup
¾ c. dry white wine or milk
½ t. dill weed
¼ t. cayenne
1 lb. medium shrimp, peeled, deveined
2 c. shredded Swiss cheese
¼ c. thinly sliced green onions
3 c. cooked rice or 3-6 English muffins, split, toasted
½ c. sliced almonds

Simmer asparagus in water to cover for 8 minutes until tender; drain; keep warm. Combine soup, wine, dill weed and cayenne; bring to a boil. Add shrimp; cover. Simmer 3-5 minutes until shrimp turn pink. Stir in cheese and onion. Arrange asparagus on top of rice or muffins; spoon shrimp mixture over all; sprinkle with almonds.

Charlotte Forristel (Mrs. Harry, Jr.)

Barbecued Shrimp

Serves 4

2 lbs. large raw shrimp, shelled, deveined
½ c. soy sauce
½ c. butter, melted
1-2 garlic cloves, mashed
½ c. chopped parsley
pepper

Place shrimp on foil-lined baking sheet. Brush with soy sauce; marinate for 15 minutes. Combine remaining ingredients; pour over shrimp. Barbecue over charcoal or broil 4″ from heat for 5 minutes.

Anne Keyko (Mrs. George)

Shrimp à la Rillo's

Serves 4

24 shrimp
1 c. flour
4 T. drawn butter
½ c. white wine
3 T. chicken base
4 T. butter
¼ c. parsley
8 slices prosciutto
8 slices mozzarella

Coat shrimp lightly with flour; saute in drawn butter. Add wine, chicken base, butter and parsley. Place in broiler pan. Top with prosciutto and mozzarella. Put under broiler for a few seconds until cheese melts. Garnish with parsley.

Rillo's Restaurant, East Hanover

Shrimp Scampi Sauce "Lunch Bunch"

Serves 4-6

3 T. Butter
2 T. minced garlic
1½ lb. raw shrimp,
   shelled and cleaned
1¼ c. heavy cream,
   divided
¼ c. dry white wine
½ c. tomato sauce
½ t. basil
½ t. oregano
2 egg yolks
2 T. minced parsley

Saute garlic in butter for 1 minute. Add shrimp; cook over medium heat, stirring until shrimp are pink. Blend in 1 cup of the cream and next four ingredients. Beat egg yolks with remaining cream; add to sauce, stirring until it thickens. Do not allow to boil. Serve over hot buttered pasta, sprinkled with parsley.

Anne Carpenter
Betty Lamborn

Pasta with Shrimp and Mushrooms

Serves 2

4 oz. thin spaghetti,
   cooked, rinsed,
   drained
½ c. butter
1 small garlic clove,
   minced
½ lb. large raw shrimp,
   cut in small pieces
½ lb. mushrooms, sliced
3 T. grated Romano
   cheese
½ t. salt
freshly ground pepper

Heat butter in large skillet. Add garlic, shrimp and mushrooms. Cook slowly for 5 minutes. Add cooked spaghetti to skillet; sprinkle with cheese, salt and pepper. Toss until spaghetti is very hot. Turn into warmed serving dish. Serve with extra Romano cheese.

Charles Langgaard, M.D.

Saucy Shrimp Squares

Serves 6

1½ c. milk
3 eggs, slightly beaten
1 t. Worcestershire
 sauce
1 t. salt
1½ c. instant rice,
 steeped in 1½ c.
 boiling water
½ 10 oz. pkg. frozen
 peas
1 4 oz. can sliced
 mushrooms
1 2 oz. jar chopped
 pimiento
1 c. shredded Cheddar
 cheese
¼ c. chopped parsley
2 4½ oz. cans shrimp,
 drained
1 can cream of shrimp
 soup
½ c. sour cream
1 t. lemon juice
salt

Combine milk, eggs, Worcestershire sauce and salt. Stir in rice, peas, mushrooms, pimiento, cheese, parsley and shrimp. Turn into a greased 7x11" pan. Bake at 325° for 55 minutes. Cut into squares. Combine remaining ingredients; heat. Serve over rice-shrimp squares.

Cornelia Keitzman (Mrs. Leo)

Curried Shrimp-Rice Salad

Serves 6

2-3 c. rice, cooked and
 chilled
1½ c. thinly sliced celery
1 10 oz. pkg. frozen
 peas, cooked
14-16 oz. shrimp, cooked
⅓ c. sliced green onions
½ c. salad oil
3 T. vinegar
1 T. soy sauce
1 t. curry powder
1 t. salt
½ t. celery seed
½ t. sugar
almonds, slivered,
 blanched and toasted
 in butter

Toss rice, celery, peas, shrimp and onions together; chill. Combine remaining ingredients except almonds; place in jar and shake to blend. At serving time, toss salad with enough dressing to moisten; sprinkle with almonds.

Julie Ann Planck (Mrs. J. Kent)

Tuna-Feta-Spinach Pie

Serves 6-8

2 10 oz. pkgs. frozen
   chopped spinach
½ c. chopped scallions
8 oz. Feta cheese,
   crumbled
1 7 oz. can tuna, drained
   and flaked
½ t. dill weed
1 9″ deep pie shell,
   unbaked or 2
   8″ pie shells
4 eggs
½ c. milk

Cook spinach just long enough to defrost; drain well. Add scallions, cheese, tuna and dill weed; mix well. Spread into pie shell. Whisk eggs and milk together until light; pour over spinach mixture. Bake at 350° for 45 minutes, until custard is set.

Lee Swenson (Mrs. C. Richard)

Tuna Ring with Cheese Sauce

Serves 6

1 egg, slightly beaten
2 7 oz. cans tuna,
   drained
½ c. chopped onion
2½ c. Cheddar cheese,
   shredded
½ c. snipped parsley
1 t. celery salt
¼ t. pepper
2 c. Bisquick
½ c. cold water
3 T. butter, melted
2 T. flour
1 t. salt
2 c. milk
½ t. Worcestershire
   sauce

Reserve 2 tablespoons of the egg. Stir tuna, onion, ½ cup of the cheese, parsley, celery salt and pepper into remaining egg. Combine Bisquick and water; knead 5 times on floured surface; roll into a 10″x15″ rectangle. Spread with tuna mixture. Roll up, starting at long side; place seam side down on a greased baking sheet; shape into a ring. With scissors, make cuts ⅔ of the way through 1″ apart; turn each section slightly to expose filling. Brush top with reserved egg. Bake at 375° for 25-30 minutes. Combine butter, flour and salt; add milk. Cook, stirring, until thickened. Add remaining cheese and Worcestershire sauce; cool, stirring until cheese melts. Pour sauce over tuna ring.

Betty Miles (Mrs. Martin)

Tuna-Rice Cakes

Serves 4

1 7 oz. can water-
   packed tuna
2 c. cooked rice
¼ c. chopped celery
1 T. chopped green
   onion
2 T. flour
¼ t. pepper
2 eggs, separated
1 c. oil
1 lemon, cut into
   wedges

Combine tuna and its liquid, rice, celery, onion, flour and pepper; add egg yolks; mix well. Fold in stiffly beaten egg whites. Heat oil in large skillet; drop in mixture by ¼ cupfuls, spreading with back of spoon to form thin cakes. Brown on each side. Garnish with lemon wedges.

Charlanne Lamberto (Mrs. Victor)

Tuna Sauce for Pasta "Lunch Bunch"

Serves 4-6

2 6½ oz. cans solid
   white tuna in oil,
   drained
2 T. butter
1 T. lemon juice
⅛ t. cayenne
2 T. finely minced
   parsley
½ c. chicken broth
salt and pepper
2 T. capers, rinsed and
   drained
1 c. heavy cream

Saute flaked tuna in butter. Add all ingredients except heavy cream; heat thoroughly. Add cream, but do not allow to boil. Serve over pasta with freshly grated Parmesan cheese.

Anne Carpenter
Betty Lamborn

Oriental Tuna Salad

Serves 4-6

½ c. mayonnaise
1 T. lemon juice
1½ t. soy sauce
garlic powder
1 7 oz. can tuna, drained
1 8 oz. can water
　 chestnuts, sliced
1 9 oz. pkg. frozen
　 Italian green beans,
　 cooked slightly
1 5 oz. can Chinese
　 noodles

Combine first four ingredients; stir in tuna, chestnuts and beans. Chill. Just before serving, add noodles.

Pi Beta Phi Alumnae Club of Northern New Jersey

Baked Bass with Tian of Vegetables

Serves 6

1 T. oil
2 T. butter
½ c. finely chopped
　 onion
1 lb. zucchini, finely
　 chopped
1 c. rice
2 c. tomatoes, chopped
salt and pepper
1½ c. chopped parsley
¼ c. chopped mint
　 leaves
2 T. lemon juice
1 4 lb. striped bass,
　 cleaned
butter
tomato and lemon slices

Saute onion in oil and butter until soft. Add zucchini; saute 3 minutes. Stir in rice and tomatoes; season with salt and pepper; bring to a boil. Cook over medium heat until rice is tender and most of liquid is absorbed, but mixture is still soupy. Add parsley, mint and 1 T. of the lemon juice. Turn into a large baking dish. Place whole fish on top; dot with butter; sprinkle with additional salt and pepper. Bake at 400° for 30-40 minutes until fish is done. Garnish with tomato and lemon slices.

Ruthelizabeth Lovretin (Mrs. Andrew)

Salmon Cured With Dill

1 3 lb. fresh salmon
4 T. crushed
   peppercorns
large bunch fresh dill
¼ c. kosher salt
¼ c. sugar

Clean and scale salmon; cut in half lengthwise; remove all bones. With hand, work half the crushed pepper into salmon. In a deep glass casserole, place half the fish skin-side down with dill on top. Sprinkle with combined salt, sugar and remaining pepper. Top with other half of fish, skin-side up. Cover with foil; weigh down evenly with a platter topped with heavy cans. Refrigerate 2-3 days, turning fish every 12 hours and basting thoroughly with marinade. To serve, remove from marinade; dry with paper towels; carve into ¼ inch slices. Garnish with lemon wedges.

The Committee

Baked Salmon Portland

Serves 6-8

1 5 lb. whole fresh
   salmon, cleaned
salt
1 c. lemon juice
3 c. saltine cracker
   crumbs
¼ c. butter, melted
½ t. salt
2 T. vinegar
1 bay leaf, crushed
1 t. Worcestershire
   sauce
2 T. chopped chives
¼ t. poultry seasoning

Rub fish inside and out with salt; sprinkle with lemon juice. Combine remaining ingredients; stuff into fish cavity. Sew or skewer together. Bake on rack in shallow pan uncovered at 350° for 1 hour.

Nancy Morrow (Mrs. David)

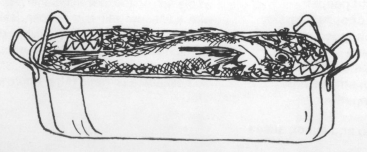

Flounder Provencale

Serves 4

1 c. chopped onion
½ c. diced celery
1 c. salad oil
1 16 oz. can tomatoes
2 T. chopped parsley
2 bay leaves
1¼ t. salt
¼ t. pepper
1 lb. flounder fillets

In large skillet, saute onion and celery in oil until tender; add tomatoes, parsley, bay leaves, salt and pepper. Simmer, covered, for 20 minutes. Add fish, spooning some of the mixture on top. Cook 10 minutes or until fish flakes.

Pat Nork (Mrs. Albert)

Fillet Florentine

Serves 6

2 10 oz. pkgs. frozen
   chopped spinach,
   cooked and drained
   (or 2 lbs. fresh)
6 sole or flounder
   fillets (about 1½ lbs.)
3 T. butter
2 T. flour
1½ c. milk
Parmesan cheese
salt and pepper

Spread spinach on bottom of baking dish. Arrange fillets on top. In top of double boiler, melt butter; add flour; stir to blend. Slowly add milk, stirring to thin white sauce consistency. Add enough cheese for medium consistency, stirring until smooth. Season with salt and pepper. Pour sauce over fish. Bake at 350° for 20 minutes; broil an additional 3-5 minutes to brown lightly.

Maureen Ogden (Mrs. Robert)

Sole Gratinée

Serves 6-8

1 T. chopped parsley
1 T. chopped chives
¼ lb. mushrooms,
   coarsley chopped
flour
bread crumbs
6-8 sole or flounder
   fillets
salt and pepper
½ c. white wine
½ c. chicken broth
Swiss or Gruyere
   cheese, grated
butter

Combine parsley, chives and mushrooms. Grease a shallow baking dish, lightly sprinkle with flour, then a thin layer of bread crumbs. Put half of the mushroom mixture in dish. Lay fillets on top of mushrooms. Sprinkle with salt and pepper; top with remaining mushroom mixture. Pour wine and broth over all. Sprinkle lightly with additional crumbs and cheese; dot with butter. Bake at 350° for 30 minutes until lightly browned.

Dorothy Graf (Mrs. George)

Roll-ups

6 bacon strips, cooked,
  crumbled (reserve fat)
4-8 oz. of pkg'd. herb-
  seasoned stuffing
butter, melted
2 T. minced parsley
¼ c. minced onion
6 flounder or sole
  fillets
milk
1 3 oz. can mushrooms,
  drained (reserve
  liquid)
1 can cream of
  mushroom soup
sherry

Combine stuffing, bacon fat and enough butter to moisten slightly; stir in bacon, parsley and onion. Spread on fillets; roll up; secure with toothpicks. Brush with additional melted butter. Bake at 375° for 30 minutes. Add enough milk to reserved mushroom liquid to measure ⅓ cup. Blend; heat with soup and sherry; pour over fish.

Lissa Anderson (Mrs. Richard)

Shrimp Stuffed Snapper

Serves 4-6

1 4 lb. red snapper
3 t. salt, divided
¾ t. pepper, divided
¾ lb. shrimp, cooked,
  cleaned
1 egg, beaten
1 T. minced onion
1 c. heavy cream,
  divided
1 T. cognac
2 T. butter

Split and bone fish. Season inside and out with 2 teaspoons salt and ½ teaspoon pepper. Finely chop shrimp; mix with egg, onion, ½ cup cream, remaining salt, pepper and cognac. Stuff fish; sew or skewer the opening. Melt butter in baking pan; add fish. Bake at 375° for 15 minutes. Add remaining cream; bake 40 minutes until fish flakes easily. Baste occasionally.

The Committee

Paella Valenciana

2 chicken breasts,
  halved
4 chicken drumsticks
4 chicken thighs
⅓ c. vegetable oil
1 c. chopped onion
1 garlic clove, minced
4 c. chicken broth
1 t. white pepper
3½ t. salt
¾ t. dried tarragon
½ t. paprika
1 t. saffron
2 c. rice, uncooked
2 c. canned tomatoes,
  drained
1½ lbs. raw shrimp,
  shelled
1 8 oz. stick of
  pepperoni, sliced
1 10 oz. pkg. frozen
  peas, cooked
12 littleneck clams,
  unshucked,
  scrubbed
12 mussels, unshucked,
  scrubbed

Saute chicken in oil until browned; remove. In pan drippings, saute onion and garlic until soft. Add broth, pepper, salt, tarragon, paprika and saffron; bring to a boil. Add rice; cook, covered, until half the liquid has been absorbed. Add tomatoes, shrimp and chicken; simmer, covered, for 30 minutes until rice is almost dry. Add pepperoni before end of cooking time to heat through. Add peas. Transfer all to large platter. Serve with clams and mussels which have been steamed in 2" boiling water for 10 minutes to open shells.

Lee Moore (Mrs. Robert)
Marion Stuart (Mrs. Russell)

Eggs, Cheese, Pasta

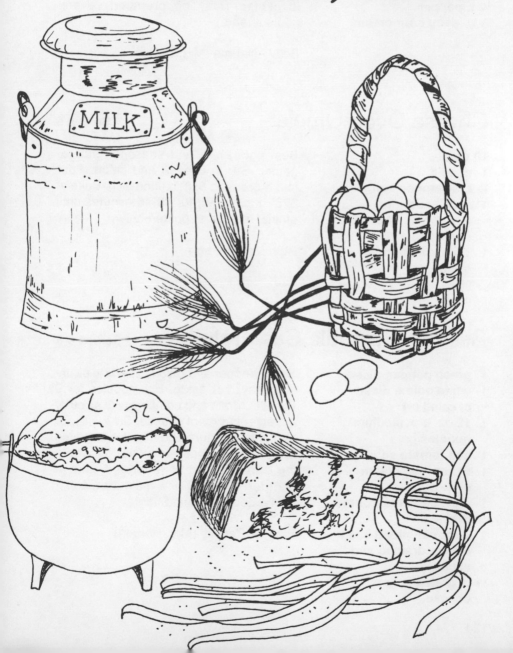

Canadian Bacon-Egg Pie

Serves 6

½ lb. Canadian bacon,
  sliced
¼ lb. Swiss cheese,
  sliced
10 large eggs, beaten
1 T. milk
¼ t. salt
¼ t. pepper
½ c. dairy sour cream

Arrange bacon on bottom of 8x8″ baking dish, overlapping pieces and letting bacon go up the sides slightly. Top with cheese. Combine eggs, milk, salt and pepper; pour over cheese. Dot with sour cream, once over each serving. Bake at 400° for 25-30 minutes until eggs are firm in center. (May be prepared several hours ahead.)

Betty Alliaume (Mrs. Curtis)

Cheese Oven Omelet

Serves 6

10 eggs
1 c. milk
½ t. seasoned salt
1½ c. Cheddar or
  mozzarella cheese,
  shredded
1 T. instant minced
  onion

Beat eggs, milk and seasoned salt together. Stir in cheese and onion. Pour into a greased 8x8″ baking dish. Bake at 325° uncovered, for 40-45 minutes until omelet is set and golden brown.

Ruth Macpherson

Best-Ever Noodle Casserole

Serves 6-8

1 green pepper, diced
1 white onion, diced
½ c. salad oil
1 12 oz. box medium
  noodles
1 can tomato soup
1 8½ oz. can cream
  style corn
1 4 oz. can mushrooms,
  drained
1 4 oz. can pitted black
  olives, drained and
  sliced
½ c. grated yellow
  cheese

Saute pepper and onions slowly in oil until glossy; set aside. Boil noodles for 9 minutes; drain and combine with all other ingredients except cheese. Stir in pepper and onion mixture and transfer to baking dish. Sprinkle cheese over all. Place baking dish in a pan of water and bake at 350° for 1 hour. (For a main dish, add 1 pound cooked ground beef.)

Eleanor Pappky (Mrs. Herbert)

Cottage Cheese Loaf

Serves 4-6

1½ c. cottage cheese
1 c. chopped walnuts
¾ c. fresh wholewheat
   breadcrumbs
1 c. finely chopped
   celery
1 medium onion, finely
   chopped
1 c. milk
3 eggs, beaten
1 T. oil
1½ t. salt
¾ t. onion salt
pinch of sweet basil
brown or mushroom
   gravy

Combine all ingredients except gravy; mix well. Bake in a well-greased, paper-lined loaf pan at 350° for 1 hour until set. Top with gravy, if desired.

Deborah Ann Sappah

Cheese and Noodle Pie

Serves 4-6

¾ c. flour, sifted
¼ t. (heaping) dry
   mustard
¾ t. salt, divided
2 c. grated Cheddar
   cheese, divided
6 T. butter, melted,
   divided
2 c. thinly sliced onion
1 c. cooked wide
   noodles
2 eggs, beaten
1 c. hot milk
pepper

Combine flour, mustard and ½ teaspoon salt; stir in half the cheese and 4 tablespoons butter. Press mixture evenly over bottom and sides of a greased 9″ pie pan. Saute onions in remaining butter; toss with noodles and spread mixture over crust. Combine eggs, milk and pepper with remaining cheese and salt. Pour into pie pan. Bake at 325° for 35-40 minutes until set.

Ann Newell (Mrs. Joseph)

Gnocchi Romaine

Serves 10-12

1 qt. milk
¾ c. butter
1 c. hominy grits
1 t. salt
⅛ t. pepper
⅓ c. melted butter
1 c. grated Gruyere
   cheese
⅓ c. Parmesan cheese

**Variation: 1½ c. grated
   sharp Cheddar cheese
   and ½ c. chopped
   scallion may be used
   in place of Gruyere
   and Parmesan**

Bring milk to a boil; add butter and gradually stir in hominy grits. Continue cooking, stirring constantly until it looks like cooked farina. Remove from heat. Add salt and pepper; beat with mixer at high speed for 5 minutes. Pour into a 13x9" baking dish and allow to set. Cut into rectangles. Place in a smaller casserole, like rows of fallen dominoes. Pour melted butter over all and sprinkle with cheeses. Bake at 400° for 30 minutes.

Kenneth D. Meals
Mary Schweikert (Mrs. Raymond)
Kay Shea (Mrs. John)

Papa's Canneloni

Serves 4-6

Pasta:
1 c. water
1 c. flour
pinch of salt
2 eggs
oil for frying

Filling:
1 lb. ricotta cheese
1 egg
½ lb. mozzarella cheese,
   shredded
chopped parsley
salt and pepper

Topping:
1 qt. Italian style tomato
   sauce
Parmesan cheese

Combine water, flour, salt and eggs; mix well with a fork and let batter stand for 20 minutes. Cover the bottom of a small skillet with oil; heat until hot. Add ⅓ cup batter; swirl in pan to make a thin crepe. When crepe looks almost dry, flip and cook another 30 seconds. Remove crepe and repeat procedure with balance of the batter, re-oiling the pan and stacking cooked crepes on a platter. Combine all filling ingredients. Spoon an equal amount of filling on each crepe; roll, folding ends in like an envelope. Pour a thin layer of sauce over bottom of a shallow baking dish. Arrange crepes in dish; pour remaining sauce over all and sprinkle with cheese. Cover and bake at 350° for 45 minutes; uncover and bake for 45 minutes more.

Sheila Duetsch (Mrs. Bernard)

Fettuccini with Spinach

Serves 4

1 clove garlic, minced
2 T. chopped onion
½ c. butter, divided
1 10 oz. pkg. frozen
  spinach, thawed,
  drained
1 8 oz. pkg. fettucini
  noodles, cooked,
  drained
½ c. heavy cream or
  milk
¾ c. Parmesan or
  Romano cheese
½ t. basil
parsley
freshly ground pepper

Saute garlic and onion in half the butter until softened; add spinach and cook for 5 minutes. Set aside. Mix remaining butter with hot cooked noodles; stir in cream, cheese and basil. Add spinach mixture; toss. Garnish with parsley and pepper.

Chris Olsen (Mrs. Charles)
Phyllis Western (Mrs. Vernon)

Eggplant Spaghetti

Serves 10-12

½ c. oil
1 large eggplant,
  unpeeled, chopped
2 medium onions,
  chopped
1 green pepper,
  chopped
½ head cauliflower,
  chopped
½ c. parsley, chopped
¼ lb. mushrooms, sliced
8 garlic cloves, minced
2 28 oz. cans tomatoes
1 15 oz. can tomato
  sauce
1 bay leaf
1 t. basil
1 t. oregano
1 t. thyme
½ t. marjoram
½ t. rosemary
salt
1 c. dry white wine
3 lbs. spaghetti
Parmesan cheese

Saute vegetables and garlic in oil for 15 minutes; stir frequently. Add tomatoes, tomato sauce and spices; bring to boil. Reduce heat and simmer 3-4 hours, adding wine as sauce thickens. Prepare spaghetti according to package directions. Pour sauce on top; sprinkle with cheese.

Kenneth D. Meals

Spaghetti Primavera

2 T. oil
4 T. butter, divided
1 pt. cherry tomatoes
2 cloves garlic, minced
½ t. salt
pepper
1 t. basil
1 lb. spaghetti
6 cups chopped
  broccoli
½ c. Parmesan cheese
¼ c. chopped parsley
½-1 c. chicken broth
½ c. chopped walnuts,
  toasted

Combine oil with half the butter; add tomatoes and cook 5 minutes. Stir in garlic, salt, pepper and basil; cook 3 minutes and set aside. Cook spaghetti according to package directions, adding broccoli during last 5 minutes. Drain and toss with remaining butter. Stir in tomatoes, cheese and parsley; add broth to moisten. Garnish with walnuts.

Brenda MacDowell (Mrs. David)

Broccoli Strata

1 10 oz. pkg. frozen
  chopped broccoli
4 slices rye or
  wholewheat bread,
  toasted
4 slices American
  cheese
½ c. chopped pimientos
4 slices Swiss cheese
4 eggs, beaten
2 c. milk
1 T. chopped onion
½ t. prepared mustard
1 t. salt
pepper
breadcrumbs
2 T. butter

Cook broccoli, covered, in boiling water for 3 minutes; drain. Arrange toast in an ungreased 9x9″ baking dish; top with American cheese, then broccoli and pimiento. Cover with Swiss cheese. Combine eggs, milk, onion, mustard, salt and pepper; pour over all. Cover and refrigerate for 1 hour. Uncover; sprinkle with bread crumbs and dot with butter. Bake, uncovered, at 350° for 1 hour until knife inserted halfway comes out clean. Let stand 10 minutes; serve.

Cathy Connell (Mrs. Robert)

Escarole Pie

Serves 6

3-4 lbs. escarole
1 c. raisins
¾ c. Pignoli nuts
½ c. vegetable oil
1 garlic clove, minced
2 c. flour
½ t. salt
1 c. shortening
1 t. paprika
½ t. garlic powder
2 egg yolks, slightly
beaten
1-2 T. water

Cook escarole; drain very well. Combine with raisins, nuts, oil and garlic. Set aside. Sift together flour and salt. Cut in shortening, paprika and garlic. Add egg yolks and water to dough. Press into 9″ pie pan. Fill crust with escarole mixture. Bake at 350° for 60 minutes.

Lawrence Nastro, M.D.

Mushroom-Cheese Bake

Serves 8

½ c. flour
2 c. milk
4½ T. butter, divided
½ t. salt
⅛ t. pepper
¼ t. nutmeg
4 eggs
1⅓ c. coarsely grated
Swiss cheese,
divided

Mushroom Filling:
1 c. finely minced fresh
mushrooms
1 T. minced scallions
1 T. melted butter
1 T. flour
4 T. heavy cream

Combine flour and milk by gradually whisking in the milk. Stir constantly over moderate heat until mixture comes to a boil and thickens. Remove from heat; beat in all but 1 tablespoon of butter, salt, pepper and nutmeg. Beat in eggs, one at a time and add 1 cup of the cheese. Turn half the mixture into a lightly buttered baking dish. Spread with Mushroom Filling; top with remaining mixture. Sprinkle with remaining cheese and dot with remaining butter. Bake at 400° for 25-30 minutes. (May be prepared a few hours ahead; bake just before serving.)

Filling: Saute mushrooms and scallions in mixture of butter and oil. Blend in flour; add cream and stir until thickened.

Teddi Kreuzer

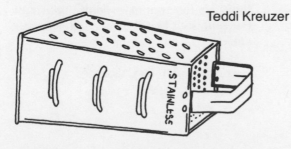

Ham and Mushroom Casserole

2 T. butter, melted
2 T. flour
1 c. milk
¼ lb. Monterey Jack
   cheese, shredded
¼ lb. mild Cheddar
   cheese, shredded
¼ lb. mozzarella cheese,
   shredded
3 lbs. cooked ham,
   thinly sliced
1 lb. mushrooms,
   sliced, sauteed

Combine butter and flour; add milk. Cook, stirring constantly for 1 minute until thickened. Add shredded cheeses; simmer, stirring frequently until cheeses have melted. Place half of the ham in a greased 9x13″ baking dish. Spread with half of the mushrooms; cover with half of the sauce. Repeat layers. Bake at 350° for 20-30 minutes until browned on top.

Liga Byrne (Mrs. Roger)

Zippy Pepperoni Pie   Serves 4

4 oz. Muenster cheese,
   shredded, divided
1 egg, beaten
¾ c. flour
¼ t. oregano
1½ t. salt
1 c. milk
¼ c. sliced pepperoni

Mix half the cheese with all other ingredients; pour mixture into greased 8″ pie plate. Bake at 425° for 25-30 minutes. Do not overcook. Sprinkle on remaining cheese; bake for 2 more minutes until cheese melts.

Suzy Gumm (Mrs. Frederick)

Zucchini Crust Pizza   Serves 4-6

3 c. grated zucchini
3 eggs, well-beaten
⅓ c. flour
¼ t. salt
2 c. grated mozzarella
   cheese
1 2½ oz. can sliced
   black olives, drained
⅔ c. minced green
   onions
½ c. minced Italian
   pickled peppers
1 t. oregano
½ t. basil
3 medium tomatoes,
   thinly sliced
salt

Press excess liquid from zucchini; combine pulp with eggs, flour and salt. Mix well; spread evenly in a greased 13x9″ baking dish. Bake at 450° for 8 minutes; remove from oven; cover zucchini base with cheese. Combine olives, onions and peppers; spoon evenly over cheese. Top with oregano and basil. Arrange tomatoes on top; sprinkle lightly with salt. Bake at 350° for 20 minutes until base is set.

Barbara Leach (Mrs. Gordon)

Tomato-Cheese Zucchini

1 onion, chopped
2 garlic cloves, minced
2 T. olive oil
½-1 lb. ground beef
1 16 oz. can whole
    tomatoes
1 6 oz. can tomato paste
1 t. oregano
¼ t. thyme
½ t. basil
salt and pepper
¾ c. red wine
4 large zucchini, cut in
    ¼″ slices
8 oz. ricotta cheese
8 oz. mozzarella cheese,
    shredded
½ c. Parmesan cheese

Saute onions and garlic in oil; add meat and brown well. Stir in tomatoes, tomato paste, oregano, thyme, basil, salt, pepper and wine. Simmer for 1½ hours. Meanwhile, parboil zucchini; drain. Arrange half of them in a deep greased baking dish. Top with half the ricotta cheese, half the mozzarella and half the sauce. Repeat layers; sprinkle with Parmesan cheese. Bake at 350° for 30 minutes.

Kathleen DeWolfe

Sandwiches

Gooey Buns

Serves 16

1 lb. bologna, shredded
¾ lb. Cheddar or
    American cheese,
    shredded
1 T. minced onion
¼ c. mustard
⅓ c. mayonnaise
2 T. pickle relish
16 hot dog buns,
    buttered

Combine all ingredients except buns. Fill buns with mixture; wrap individually in foil. Bake at 300° for 25 minutes. May be frozen.

Lucille Mayer (Mrs. John)

Caraccas

Serves 2-3

1 1 lb. can tomatoes,
    undrained
1 2½ oz. jar dried beef
1½ c. grated Cheddar
    cheese
1 T. onion juice
2 eggs, beaten

Chop tomatoes. Rinse beef; tear into bite size pieces. Mix all together. Heat slowly, stirring constantly until it boils. Serve on toast.

Cathy Connell (Mrs. Robert)

Barbecued Chicken

Serves 30

2½ c. chicken broth
flour
water
¼ c. sugar
2 T. mustard
salt and pepper
1 4 oz. jar chopped
    pimiento
1 medium onion,
    chopped
1 14 oz. bottle ketchup
meat of 3 medium
    chickens, cooked, finely
    chopped
30 hamburger buns

Thicken broth with a mixture of flour and water; add remaining ingredients except chicken; cook until thickened. Add chicken. Spoon into buns.

Ann Newell (Mrs. Joseph)

Hot Browns

Serves 4

1 medium onion, chopped
⅓ c. + 1 T. butter, melted
⅓ c. flour
3 c. milk, heated
1 t. salt
⅛ t. crushed red pepper
¼ lb. processed cheese, cubed
2 eggs, beaten
8 slices white bread, toasted, cut in half diagonally
sliced cooked chicken or turkey
sliced cooked ham
tomato slices
8 bacon strips, cooked
Parmesan cheese
paprika
sauteed mushroom caps

Cook onion in ⅓ cup butter until clear. Blend in flour; add milk, salt and pepper. Cook, stirring, until thickened and smooth. Add cheese, eggs and remaining butter. (As a substitute for the above, frozen Welsh rarebit may be used). Place 8 toast points on each of 4 ovenproof plates; place ham and chicken slices on top. Cover with sauce; top with tomato slices and bacon; sprinkle with cheese and paprika. Broil until sauce bubbles. Garnish with mushroom caps.

Kay Shea (Mrs. John)
Kekee Szorcsik (Mrs. J. Mitchell)

Hot Spicy Ham Sandwiches

Serves 8

¼ lb. butter, softened
2 T. poppy seeds
⅓ c. chopped onion
⅓ c. mustard
8 hard rolls or hamburger buns
8 slices Swiss cheese
8 slices cooked ham

Combine butter, poppy seeds, onion and mustard; spread on both sides of buns. Place one slice ham and one slice cheese between bun halves; wrap individually in foil. Bake at 350° for 15 minutes.

Jeanne Kennedy (Mrs. John)
Kekee Szorcsik (Mrs. J. Mitchell)

Hound Dogs

½ lb. sharp Cheddar
  cheese, cubed
½ lb. cooked ham, cubed
⅓ c. chopped onion
2 eggs, hard-cooked,
  chopped
½ c. thinly sliced green
  onions
2 T. mayonnaise
½ c. chili sauce
12-14 hot dog buns

Combine all ingredients except buns. Fill buns with mixture; wrap individually in foil. Bake at 400° for 10-15 minutes.

Faye Ericson (Mrs. Grant)

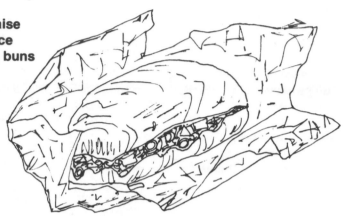

Sunburst Crab Muffins

Serves 6

½ lb. canned or frozen
  crabmeat
1 medium celery stalk,
  diced
¼ c. mayonnaise
2 t. lemon juice
⅛ t. lemon-pepper
  seasoning
¼ c. sliced almonds
3 English muffins, split,
  toasted, buttered
1 10 oz. pkg. frozen
  asparagus, cooked
3 American cheese
  slices, quartered
  diagonally
paprika

Combine first 6 ingredients; spread on muffin halves. Place asparagus on top; lay 2 cheese triangles on each; sprinkle with paprika. Bake at 400° for 15 minutes until cheese melts and bubbles.

Charlotte Forristel (Mrs. Harry Jr.)

Liverwurst and Bacon on Rye

Serves 6

6 slices rye bread,
  toasted on one side,
  buttered
18 slices liverwurst
6 bacon slices, crisply
  cooked, fat reserved
2 c. sliced fresh
  mushrooms
1 c. sliced red onion

Place bread slices untoasted side up on cookie sheet; lay 3 slices liverwurst and 1 bacon slice on each. Saute mushrooms and onion in bacon fat until soft; spread over liverwurst. Broil 4″ from heat for 3-5 minutes until lightly browned.

Nancy Morrow (Mrs. David)

Open Avocado Shrimpwich

Serves 6

1 8 oz. pkg. cream
  cheese, softened
2 T. mayonnaise
2 T. mustard
¼ t. salt
¼ t. dill weed
1 T. chopped green
  onion
6 slices rye bread,
  toasted
2 4½ oz. cans small
  shrimp
2 large avocados

Cut avocados in half crosswise. Remove seed; slice into rings; carefully peel away skin. Set aside.

Blend cream cheese, mayonnaise, mustard, salt, dill weed and onion together; spread 3 tablespoons on each bread slice. Top with shrimp and avocado rings; sprinkle with additional dill weed.

Carolyn Walters

Crunchy Health Spread

Serves 4

1 c. dry roasted soy
   nuts, finely chopped
1 medium carrot,
   shredded
2 T. raisins
¼ c. mayonnaise
3 T. honey
¼ t. salt
8 slices bread (date-nut,
   pumpernickel, rye or
   branola)

Mix all ingredients except bread. Spread on bread slices.

Charlanne Lamberto (Mrs. Victor)

Hot Tuna Sandwiches

Serves 6

¼ lb. Cheddar cheese,
   grated
3 eggs, hard-cooked,
   chopped
1 7 oz. can tuna, drained
2 T. chopped green
   pepper
2 T. chopped onion
2 T. chopped green
   olives
2 T. sweet pickle relish
½ c. mayonnaise

Combine all ingredients; spoon into six hot dog buns. Wrap individually in foil. Bake at 250° for 30 minutes.

Ann Newell (Mrs. Joseph)

Tuna Puffs

Serves 6

1 7 oz. can tuna,
   drained, flaked
1½ t. mustard
¼ t. Worcestershire
   sauce
¼ c. mayonnaise
1½ t. grated onion
2 T. chopped green
   pepper
3 hamburger buns, split
6 tomato slices
½ c. mayonnaise
¼ c. finely shredded
   American cheese

Combine first 6 ingredients; spread on 6 bun halves; top each with a tomato slice. Combine mayonnaise and cheese; spread on top of tomato slices. Broil 4″ from heat until puffy and lightly browned.

Sue Batting (Mrs. William)

Tuna Souffles

Serves 8

4 English muffins, split
½ c. margarine, divided
1 c. sliced fresh
   mushrooms
¼ c. chopped onion
1 7 oz. can tuna,
   drained, flaked
¼ c. mayonnaise
2 eggs, separated
2 c. grated Swiss
   cheese
¼ t. pepper
¼ t. cayenne

Brush muffins with ¼ cup of the margarine; broil on cookie sheet for 3-4 minutes until lightly browned. In remaining margarine, saute mushrooms and onion until golden. Add tuna; stir in mayonnaise. Spread on muffin halves. Combine egg yolks, cheese, pepper and cayenne; fold in stiffly beaten egg whites. Spoon over tuna. Bake at 375° for 12-15 minutes until cheese is puffed and firm.

Nancy Morrow (Mrs. David)

Pitawich

2 16 oz. cans white
   kidney beans, drained
5 T. oil
2 T. lemon juice
1 t. oregano
½ t. salt
½ t. ground cumin
¼ t. pepper
1 3 oz. pkg. cream
   cheese, cubed
2 medium tomatoes,
   chopped
1 cucumber, peeled,
   diced
4 small pita breads,
   halved
2 T. chopped parsley

Combine beans, oil, lemon juice, oregano, salt, cumin and pepper. Stir in cheese, tomatoes and cucumber. Cover; chill 2 hours. Fill each pita half with ⅔ cup bean mixture; sprinkle each with parsley.

Charlanne Lamberto (Mrs. Victor)

Vegetables

Artichoke Heart Surprise

Serves 6

2 9 oz. pkgs. frozen
    artichoke hearts
1 T. lemon juice
1 T. butter
¼ t. salt
¼ t. pepper
1 10 oz. pkg. frozen
    chopped broccoli
1 onion, diced
1 c. cream sauce
2 T. Parmesan cheese

Cook artichokes until barely tender; season with lemon juice, butter, salt and pepper. Place in a shallow baking dish; set aside. Cook broccoli with onion; puree in blender with cream sauce and cheese; correct seasoning if needed. Spread puree over artichokes; bake at 375° for 20 minutes.

Nancy Morrow (Mrs. David)

Walnut Broccoli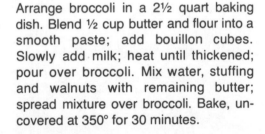

Serves 8-10

2 10 oz. pkgs. frozen
    chopped broccoli,
    thawed
½ c. plus 6 T. butter,
    melted
4 T. flour
4 chicken bouillon
    cubes, crushed
2 c. milk
⅔ c. water
⅔ of 8 oz. pkg. stuffing
    mix
¾ c. coarsely chopped
    walnuts

Arrange broccoli in a 2½ quart baking dish. Blend ½ cup butter and flour into a smooth paste; add bouillon cubes. Slowly add milk; heat until thickened; pour over broccoli. Mix water, stuffing and walnuts with remaining butter; spread mixture over broccoli. Bake, uncovered at 350° for 30 minutes.

Dorothy Royer (Mrs. Robert)
Barbara Williams (Mrs. James)

Italian Broccoli Casserole

Serves 8

1 20 oz. pkg. frozen
   broccoli, cooked and
   drained
1 8 oz. can stewed
   tomatoes, chopped
2 eggs, beaten
1 can Cheddar cheese
   soup
½ t. oregano
3 T. Parmesan cheese

Mix broccoli and tomatoes; put in a 2½ quart baking dish. Combine eggs, soup and oregano; pour over vegetables. Sprinkle with cheese. Bake uncovered at 350° for 30 minutes.

Patricia Ellis (Mrs. Roy)

Baked Beans

Serves 6

¼ lb. bacon
½ c. minced green
   pepper
½ c. minced onion
½ c. minced celery
1 20 oz. can Campbell's
   baked beans
4 T. ketchup
2 T. molasses
2 T. brown sugar
3 drops Tabasco

Fry and crumble bacon; reserve grease. Sauté pepper, onion and celery in grease; add all other ingredients including bacon. Transfer to a 2 quart baking dish; bake at 375° for 45 minutes to 1 hour.

Lib Kuhn (Mrs. Jean)

Cowboy Beans

Serves 6-8

½ lb. bacon, chopped,
   fried, drained
2 small onions,
   chopped, sauteed
1 1 lb. can baked beans
   in tomato sauce
1 1 lb. can red kidney
   beans
1 1 lb. can large lima
   beans, drained
4 oz. Cheddar cheese,
   cubed
½ c. brown sugar
¼ c. ketchup
2 T. Worcestershire sauce

Combine all ingredients. Bake in a shallow baking dish at 350° until hot and bubbly; reduce heat to 150-200° until ready to serve. (Adding bite-sized pieces of cooked Italian sweet sausage turns this into a main course dish.)

Julia Clevett (Mrs. Kenneth)
Dorothy Groner (Mrs. Walter)

Pennsylvania Dutch Green Beans

Serves 4

¾ lb. fresh green beans
1 t. salt, divided
¼ c. water
8 slices bacon, diced
2 medium potatoes, pared, cut in ½" slices
1 small onion, sliced

Cook beans with ½ teaspoon salt in boiling water for 10-15 minutes until just tender. Fry the bacon; add potatoes, onions and remaining salt. Cook 15 minutes more until potatoes are tender. Add drained cooked beans.

Dotti Sobin (Mrs. Edward)

Swiss Green Beans

Serves 8

1½-2 lbs. fresh green beans, cut
½ t. grated onion
2 T. butter, melted
2 T. flour
½ t. sugar
½ t. salt
dash pepper
½ c. milk
½ c. sour cream
1 c. shredded Swiss cheese
⅓ c. corn flake crumbs
1 T. melted butter

Cook beans until barely tender; drain and set aside. Lightly saute onion in butter; blend in flour, sugar, salt and pepper. Add milk; cook until thick and bubbly. Remove from heat; stir in sour cream and beans. Layer ⅓ of the beans in a 1 quart baking dish; sprinkle half the cheese over the beans. Repeat layers, ending with the beans. Top with corn flake crumbs mixed with butter. Bake at 400° for 20 minutes.

Karen Pfister (Mrs. Jeffrey)

Brussels Sprouts and Potatoes

Serves 6

2 10 oz. pkg. frozen Brussels sprouts or 4 cups fresh Brussels sprouts
2 beef bouillon cubes
1 small onion, minced
2 T. butter
½ c. pecan halves
½ t. Worcestershire sauce
1 c. cooked diced potatoes

Prepare sprouts according to package directions, adding bouillon cubes to liquid. Saute onion in butter until golden. Add pecans and cook, stirring, for a few seconds. Add remaining ingredients. Toss with drained sprouts.

Eleanor Pappky (Mrs. Herbert)

Deluxe Carrots

Serves 6-8

2½ lbs. carrots, julienned
salt and pepper
½ c. mayonnaise
1 T. minced onion
1 T. horseradish
1 T. mustard
2 T. butter, softened
¼ c. crumbled Ritz
   crackers
chopped parsley
paprika

Cook carrots; drain, reserving liquid. Put carrots in a baking dish; add salt and pepper. Cover with a mixture of the next 5 ingredients and reserved liquid. Top with crackers, parsley and paprika; bake at 375° for 15-20 minutes.

Gwen Moore (Mrs. David)

Copper Pennies

Serves 8-10

8-10 carrots, sliced,
   crisp-cooked
1 c. sliced celery
1 onion, thinly sliced
1 green pepper,
   chopped
1 can tomato soup
⅓ c. oil
¼ c. vinegar
½ c. sugar
1 t. dry mustard
1 t. Worcestershire
   sauce

Combine carrots, celery, onion and pepper. Bring all other ingredients to a boil; pour over vegetables. Refrigerate several hours; serve cold. Keeps several weeks.

Ann Newell (Mrs. Joseph)
Dorothy Stevens (Mrs. Charles)
Dotty Stevens (Mrs. Roger)

Curried Cauliflower

Serves 6-8

1 large head fresh
   cauliflower
½ t. salt
1 can cream of chicken
   soup
4 oz. Cheddar cheese,
   grated
⅓ c. mayonnaise
1 t. curry powder
¼ c. dried bread crumbs
2 T. butter, melted

Break cauliflower into flowerets; cook in boiling salted water for 10 minutes; drain. Mix soup, cheese, mayonnaise and curry together; stir in cauliflower; spoon into a 2½ quart baking dish. Toss bread crumbs with butter; sprinkle on top. Bake uncovered at 350° for 30 minutes.

Diane Eknoian (Mrs. Robert)

Cauliflower Stuffed Tomatoes

Serves 8

8 large tomatoes
salt
1 large head cauliflower
  separated into
  flowerets
3 T. tarragon vinegar
3 T. dry white wine
3 T. minced shallots
1 T. heavy cream
3 large egg yolks, lightly
  beaten
1 c. butter, melted
lemon juice
salt and white pepper
minced fresh parsley

Cut tops off tomatoes in decorative cuts. Scoop out pulp; sprinkle insides with salt. Drain, inverted, for 30 minutes. Cook cauliflower until just tender; drain and keep warm. Heat vinegar, wine and shallots together until liquid is reduced to 1 tablespoon; remove from heat. Stir in cream and eggs; heat slowly, whisking, until sauce thickens. Add butter, 2 tablespoons at a time, whisking, until sauce thickens. Strain through a fine sieve into top of a double boiler; stir in lemon juice, salt and white pepper. Cover with a buttered round of waxed paper; keep warm. (Can be prepared in advance up to this point.) To serve, fill tomatoes with hot cauliflower; top with warm sauce; garnish with parsley.

Summit, New Providence, Berkeley Heights Welcome Wagon

Cauliflower-Broccoli Duet

Serves 12

1 head fresh cauliflower
2 bunches fresh
  broccoli
1 pt. sour cream
8 oz. Cheddar cheese,
  grated
½ c. chicken broth
1 t. prepared mustard
¾ c. dried bread crumbs
¼ lb. butter, melted
¾ c. slivered almonds

Break cauliflower and broccoli into flowerets; parboil; drain. Arrange in a large greased baking dish; stir in mixture of sour cream, cheese, broth and mustard. Toss bread crumbs with butter; sprinkle on top, along with almonds. Bake at 325° for 30 minutes.

Pi Beta Phi Alumnae Club of
Northern New Jersey

Oriental Celery

Serves 6

4 c. diagonally sliced
  celery, parboiled and
  drained
1 8 oz. can water
  chestnuts, drained
  and thinly sliced
1 can cream of chicken
  soup
¼ c. diced pimiento
½ c. fresh bread crumbs
¼ c. toasted slivered
  almonds
2 T. melted butter

Combine all ingredients except crumbs, almonds and butter in a 1½ qt. greased baking dish. Toss remaining ingredients together; sprinkle over all. Bake at 350° for 35 minutes until heated through.

Margit Brown
Cornelia Kietzman (Mrs. Leo)
Gail Martin (Mrs. James)
Joan Murphy (Mrs. Edward)
Marion Neppl (Mrs. Walter)

Creole Stuffed Eggplant

Serves 4

1 medium eggplant
  (1¼ lbs.)
½ c. breadcrumbs
5 T. butter, divided
2 large whole scallions,
  finely chopped
2 T. chopped parsley
½ lb. fresh lump
  crabmeat or diced
  raw shrimp
¼ t. salt
¼ t. pepper
2 dashes Tabasco
2 T. Parmesan cheese

Boil eggplant for 20 minutes; drain. When cool enough to handle, cut lengthwise and carefully remove pulp, leaving a ¼" thick shell. Chop and reserve pulp. Saute scallions and parsley in 4 tablespoons butter for 2 minutes. Add crab or shrimp, stirring for 3 minutes or longer, being careful to preserve crab in lumps. Add pulp, sprinkle with salt, pepper and Tabasco. Cover; cook over low heat for 5 minutes. Pile mixture into eggplant shells in shallow baking dish. Brown bread crumbs in remaining butter; add cheese. Sprinkle over eggplant; dot each portion with butter. Bake at 350° for 20 minutes.

Lee Cowell (Mrs. John)

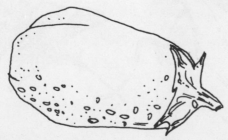

Creamy Stuffed Mushrooms

Serves 4

1 lb. mushrooms
1 c. finely chopped
   pecans
3 T. chopped parsley
¼ c. butter, softened
1 garlic clove, crushed
¼ t. ground thyme
½ t. salt
pepper
½ c. heavy cream

Remove and chop mushroom stems. Place caps in a shallow baking dish, hollow side up. Stuff, heaping with a mixture of chopped stems and all other ingredients except cream. Pour cream over caps and bake at 350° for 20 minutes, basting once or twice.

Marjorie Booth

Braised Onions

Serves 4-6

2 c. sliced onions
3 T. butter
½ t. sugar
1 t. salt
½ c. red wine

Saute onions in butter until soft; add sugar, salt and wine. Simmer for 10 minutes. (Good with steak.)

Candy Sperco (Mrs. C.J.)

Peas With Mint

Serves 12

3 10 oz. pkgs. frozen
   peas
1 t. sugar
2 8 oz. cans water
   chestnuts, drained,
   sliced
1½ T. chopped mint
   leaves
¼ c. Grand Marnier
⅓ c. butter
1 t. salt

Place peas and sugar in 1 cup boiling water; simmer 5 minutes; drain. Toss with remaining ingredients.

Judy Davies (Mrs. Robert)

Chateau Potatoes

potatoes
salt
pepper
butter
parsley

Cut raw potatoes into balls with melon scoop. Soak in cold water until ready to cook. Drain well. Season with salt and pepper. Cook slowly in skillet with generous amount of butter until golden crusty on the outside and soft inside. Sprinkle with parsley.

Eleanor Pappky (Mrs. Herbert)

Skillet New Potatoes   Serves 4

2 T. butter
2 T. oil
2 lbs. small new
   potatoes
1-2 large unpeeled garlic
   cloves
½ t. salt
pepper

Combine all ingredients in a heavy skillet. Cover; cook over low heat or on grill over hot coals 40-60 minutes until potatoes are browned and tender. Shake pan occasionally. Correct seasoning and discard garlic before serving.

Eleanor Pappky (Mrs. Herbert)

Pennsylvania Dutch Potato Filling   Serves 4-6

6-8 medium large
   potatoes
2 stalks celery, finely
   chopped
1 small onion, finely
   chopped
3 slices stale bread,
   cubed
4 T. butter
1 c. milk
2 eggs
1 T. parsley
¼ t. pepper
salt

Saute celery and onion in butter. Add bread cubes to pan to soak up juices. Cook and mash potatoes. Beat in milk and eggs. Add parsley and seasonings. Stir in celery, onion and bread. Bake in a greased casserole at 375° for 30-45 minutes until puffy and lightly browned. (Serve with turkey in place of stuffing.)

Joanne Keith (Mrs. James)

Cranberry Sweet Potatoes

4-6 Servings

4 **large sweet potatoes, cooked, peeled, cut into ¼ inch slices**
½ **c. packed light brown sugar**
2 **T. butter**
1 **c. fresh cranberries**
½ **c. orange juice**

Walnut Topping:
½ **c. chopped walnuts**
2 **T. melted butter**
1 **T. brown sugar**
½ **t. cinnamon**

Arrange half the potatoes in a 1½ quart baking dish. Sprinkle with half the sugar; dot with half the butter and top with half the cranberries. Repeat layers; pour juice over all. Cover; bake at 350° for 45 minutes. Uncover, spread with Walnut Topping; bake 10 minutes more.

Betty Miles (Mrs. Martin)

Apple Sweet Potatoes

Serves 6

3 **medium sweet potatoes**
½ **c. butter**
¾ **c. light brown sugar, packed**
½ **c. apple cider**
½ **t. mace**
¼ **t. salt**
1 **lg. apple, pared, thinly sliced**

Cook potatoes until tender. Peel, slice ¼ inch thick. Melt butter; add everything but apple. Bring to a boil, stirring until sugar is dissolved. Simmer 10 minutes. In shallow 2 quart casserole, alternately layer potato and apple slices. Spoon over half of syrup. Bake, covered, at 400° for 25 minutes. Uncover; add remaining syrup. Bake, uncovered, for 20 minutes until glazed.

Marjorie Booth
Pam Bess (Mrs. Stanley)

Spinach Patties

1 10 oz. pkg. frozen
  chopped spinach,
  cooked, drained
¼ c. Parmesan cheese
½ c. + 3 T. dried bread
  crumbs
1 egg, beaten
salt and pepper
¼ c. butter
¼ c. chopped onion

Combine spinach, cheese, 3 T. bread crumbs, egg, salt and pepper. Saute onion in butter; strain butter over spinach; discard onions. Mix well; shape into 2 inch round patties, ½ inch thick; coat well with remaining bread crumbs. Saute in oil 5 minutes on each side until heated through and crispy outside. Serve hot or cold.

Lee Moore (Mrs. Robert)

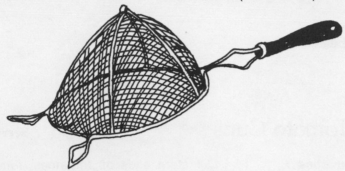

Springtime Spinach Loaf

Serves 8-10

4 eggs, lightly beaten
1 c. half and half
1 t. salt
⅛ t. pepper
¼ t. nutmeg
2 10 oz. pkgs. frozen
  chopped spinach,
  thawed, drained
½ c. chopped green
  onion, sauteed
⅔ c. dried bread crumbs
½ c. Parmesan cheese

Mushroom Sauce:
3 T. butter, melted
3 T. flour
1 c. half and half
salt and pepper
8 oz. fresh mushrooms,
  sliced, sauteed

Combine all ingredients; put in greased loaf pan. Set loaf pan in a baking dish with 2 inches of hot water; bake at 350° for 1 hour until inserted knife comes out clean. Let stand 10 minutes; unmold; serve with Mushroom Sauce.

Sauce: Blend butter, flour, cream, salt and pepper; stir in mushrooms.

Marilyn Van Slyke (Mrs. Irving)

Spinach Torte

3 10 oz. pkg. frozen
   chopped spinach,
   thawed, drained
2 c. dried bread crumbs
1½ c. Parmesan cheese
1 c. olive oil
1 c. chopped parsley
2 onions, finely
   chopped
2 garlic cloves, minced
1½ t. Italian seasonings
2 t. salt
2 t. pepper
10 eggs, beaten

Beat all ingredients together by hand for 3 minutes. Fill to half way, greased 9x13" baking dish plus 8" square baking dish. Bake at 325° for 40 minutes; cut into squares and serve hot or cold. (May be frozen and re-heated.)

Patty Proctor (Mrs. Richard)

Corn Tomato Cups

6 large tomatoes
salt
2 10 oz. pkgs. frozen
   corn, cooked, drained
1 c. grated Cheddar
   cheese
3 T. butter, melted
3 T. Parmesan cheese

Cut stem ends off tomatoes, remove pulp; sprinkle with salt; invert to drain. Stuff with mixture of corn, Cheddar cheese and butter; top with Parmesan cheese. Bake in a shallow baking dish at 350° for 20-25 minutes.

Charlanne Lamberto (Mrs. Victor)

Half-Baked Tomatoes

6 tomatoes, halved
3 T. chopped scallions
2 T. dried basil
2 T. chopped parsley
⅛ t. thyme
½ t. salt
⅛ t. pepper
¼ c. olive oil
½ c. dried bread crumbs
2 T. Parmesan cheese

Scoop out tomatoes; set shells aside; mix pulp with all other ingredients. Fill shells with mixture. Bake in a shallow baking dish at 350° for 10-15 minutes.

Maryalice Marakas (Mrs. James)

Scalloped Tomatoes and Artichokes

Serves 6-8

½ c. finely chopped
    onion
2 T. finely chopped
    shallots
¼ lb. butter
1 35 oz. can whole plum
    tomatoes, drained
1 14 oz. can artichoke
    hearts, drained and
    quartered
½ t. basil
salt and pepper
2 T. sugar

Saute onions and shallots in butter until tender; add tomatoes, artichokes and basil. Heat 2-3 minutes, stirring gently. Add salt, pepper and sugar. Spoon into greased shallow baking dish; bake at 325° for 15 minutes until heated through.

Polly Gleason (Mrs. Jack)

Mushroom Stuffed Tomatoes

Serves 8

8 firm ripe tomatoes
¼ lb. butter
1¼ lbs. mushrooms,
    sliced
1 c. sour cream
4 t. flour
3 oz. Roquefort cheese
¼ t. fines herbes
1 t. chopped parsley
2 T. dry sherry
salt and pepper
sesame seeds
    paprika

Cut a slice from top of each tomato; carefully scoop out pulp. Turn shells upside down to drain. Saute mushrooms in butter until all moisture has evaporated. Mix sour cream with flour; stir into the mushrooms over low heat until thick and bubbly. Stir in Roquefort, fines herbes, parsley, sherry, salt and pepper to taste. Cool. Loosely stuff the tomatoes. Sprinkle tops with sesame seeds and a dash of paprika. Bake at 375° for 15 minutes until bubbly.

The Committee

Summer Surprise

Serves 4

7 large tomatoes,
    peeled, seeded, cut in
    firm pieces
1 small onion, grated
2 T. parsley, minced
5 T. mayonnaise
1 t. curry powder
salt and pepper

Combine all ingredients; chill in freezer until slightly frozen. Serve in small bowls.

Constance Olinder (Mrs. Everett)

Squash Souffle

Serves 6

3 T. butter
1 c. hot milk
1½ c. dry bread crumbs,
   divided
2 lbs. yellow squash,
   cooked, mashed
1 pkg. onion soup (not
   "cup of soup")
salt and pepper
2 eggs, beaten
½ c. grated Cheddar
   cheese

Melt butter in milk; mix with one cup bread crumbs. Combine with squash, soup mix, salt and pepper. Add eggs; pour into greased baking dish. Top with remaining bread crumbs; sprinkle with cheese. Bake at 300° for 30-40 minutes until firm.

Jane Betteridge (Mrs. William)

Swiss-style Zucchini

Serves 6

1 large red onion, sliced
   in thin rings
3 c. thinly sliced
   zucchini
¼ c. butter
2 eggs, beaten
¼ c. milk
1 t. salt
⅛ t. pepper
½ t. dry mustard
1 c. grated Swiss
   cheese, divided

Saute onion and zucchini in butter until tender; place in a shallow 1½ quart baking dish. Combine all other ingredients except half the cheese; pour over zucchini. Top with remaining cheese; bake at 375° for 20 minutes until firm.

Peggy Bull (Mrs. Richard)

Zucchini Fritatta

Serves 6-8

oil
1 clove garlic, minced
1 medium onion,
   chopped
3 zucchini, thinly sliced
salt and pepper
6 eggs
2-3 T. sour cream
6 T. water
1 c. grated Swiss
   cheese
½ c. Parmesan cheese
chopped parsley

Coat a 10½" earthenware dish with oil. Put dish in a 250° oven to warm. In a separate pan, saute garlic and onion until clear. Add zucchini seasoned with salt and pepper. Cook until tender. In a bowl beat together eggs, sour cream and water. Pour into heated dish. Add sauteed vegetables. Sprinkle with cheeses. Top with parsley. Bake at 375° for 12-15 minutes.

Anne Lyon (Mrs. Richard)

Zucchini Cheddar Bake

Serves 10-12

8 slices bacon, diced
1 large onion, chopped
1 large garlic clove,
minced
7-8 zucchini, cut in ¼"
slices, cooked and
drained
4 slices white bread,
cubed
2 c. shredded Cheddar
cheese
1 t. oregano
1 t. salt
dash pepper
1 15 oz. can tomato
sauce
¼ c. Parmesan cheese

Fry bacon until crisp; remove. Saute onion and garlic in bacon fat; drain. Combine with zucchini, bacon and all other ingredients except Parmesan cheese. Spoon into a 13x9" baking dish; sprinkle with Parmesan cheese. Bake at 350° for 20 minutes until bubbly.

Marj McCaulley (Mrs. Samuel)

Crisp Zucchini Fingers

Serves 8-10

1 c. dry bread crumbs
1 t. salt
1 t. basil
1 t. tarragon
½ t. onion powder
¼ t. pepper
1 egg, beaten
2 T. lemon juice
4 medium zucchini

Hollandaise Sauce:
1 c. butter
4 egg yolks
2 T. lemon juice
⅛ t. salt
dash cayenne

Combine first six ingredients in a plastic bag. Mix egg with lemon juice. Cut zucchini into 2-3 inch pieces. Dip zucchini in egg mixture, then drop in bag and coat with bread crumbs. Place in lightly greased shallow baking pan. Bake at 350° for 30-40 minutes until zucchini is tender and browned.

Hollandaise Sauce:
Heat butter until bubbly in saucepan. Combine remaining ingredients in blender. With blender running, add hot butter in a slow stream.

Eleanor Pappky (Mrs. Herbert)

Zucchini al Forno

Serves 4-6

4 small zucchini, sliced
1 onion, thinly sliced
2 tomatoes, thinly sliced
5 slices bacon, semi-crisp, crumbled
8 oz. mozzarella cheese, thinly sliced
garlic salt
oregano

In a 3 quart baking dish, layer ⅓ of each ingredient beginning with zucchini and ending with seasonings. Repeat twice more. Cover; bake at 350° for 1½ hours.

Ann Newell (Mrs. Joseph)

Garden Medley

Serves 6

2 T. vegetable oil
1 onion, sliced
1 garlic clove, minced
¼ c. minced fresh parsley
2 t. salt
¼ t. pepper
¼ t. ground thyme
¼ t. sage
1 lb. fresh green or wax beans
3 fresh tomatoes, diced
2 c. diced fresh yellow squash

Saute in oil for 3 minutes all ingredients except beans, tomatoes and squash. Mix in the beans, tomatoes and squash; add water to ⅓ the depth of the mixture. Cover; simmer 20 minutes.

Ann Brown (Mrs. William)

Ratatouille

Serves 6-8

1 eggplant, unpeeled and cubed
oil
5 tomatoes, peeled and sliced
1 garlic clove, chopped
1 T. flour
salt and pepper

Lightly saute ⅓ of the eggplant at a time in oil. While cooking, sprinkle with part of the garlic and flour; gradually add ⅓ of the tomatoes. Repeat until all ingredients except seasonings are used. Season with salt and pepper; bake in a covered baking dish at 350° until eggplant is tender. Serve hot or cold. Mixture may instead be cooked in a covered skillet on range top.

Variation: Include sliced mushrooms or add grated Parmesan cheese topping.

Millicent Fenwick

Curried Vegetables with Brown Rice

Serves 6

4 tomatoes, sliced
3 zucchini, sliced
1 onion, sliced
2 vegetable bouillon
   cubes dissolved in ¾
   c. water
3 T. oil
2 t. curry powder
½ t. salt
¼ t. pepper
2 16 oz. cans chick
   peas, drained
2 T. flour blended with ¼
   c. water
3 c. cooked brown rice

In a covered skillet, cook tomatoes, zucchini and onion in a mixture of bouillon, oil, curry, salt and pepper until zucchini is barely tender. Add chick peas; simmer 5 minutes. Add flour and water mixture; stir and cook until thickened. Serve with brown rice.

Charlanne Lamberto (Mrs. Victor)

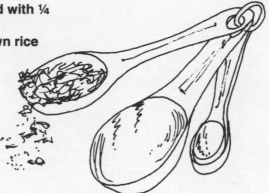

Breads

Applesauce Raisin Bread

Yield: 1 loaf

1½ c. flour, sifted
1 t. baking soda
1 t. baking powder
1 t. salt
1 t. cinnamon
1 t. nutmeg
½ t. allspice
½ t. ground cloves
1 c. oats
½ c. brown sugar
2 eggs
⅓ c. oil
1 c. applesauce
1 c. raisins

Combine dry ingredients; add remaining ingredients, stirring by hand until all ingredients are moistened. Pour into a greased 8x4″ loaf pan. Bake at 350° for 1 hour.

Janelle Tate

Apricot Wheat Bread

Yield: 1 loaf

1½ c. dried apricots, finely chopped
1 8¼ oz. can crushed pineapple
1 c. light brown sugar, firmly packed, divided
½ c. margarine
2 c. sifted flour
2 t. baking powder
½ t. salt
5 large shredded wheat biscuits, crumbled
¾ c. chopped walnuts
2 eggs, beaten
¾ c. milk

Simmer apricots, pineapple and ¼ cup brown sugar for 10 minutes, stirring occasionally. Add margarine, stirring to melt; cool. Add sifted dry ingredients. Mix in remaining brown sugar, biscuit crumbs and nuts. Stir in eggs, milk and fruit mixture. Turn into greased 9x5″ loaf pan; bake at 350° for 1-1¼ hours; cool on rack. Loaf will not rise.

Jean Fiory (Mrs. Anthony)

Sour Cream-Banana Bread

Yield: 1 loaf

1 c. sugar
2 eggs, slightly beaten
½ c. butter
1 t. vanilla
1½ c. flour
1 t. baking soda
1 t. salt
1 c. mashed bananas
½ c. sour cream
½ c. chopped nuts

Cream sugar, eggs, butter and vanilla; add sifted dry ingredients; stir in bananas, sour cream and nuts. Turn into greased 9x5" loaf pan; bake at 350° for 1 hour. May be frozen.

Jacqueline Poradek (Mrs. James)

Cranberry Bread

Yield: 1 loaf

1 c. sugar
2 T. shortening
1 egg
2 c. flour
1½ t. baking powder
½ t. salt
½ t. baking soda
grated rind of 1 orange
juice of 1 orange
   combined with water
   to equal ¾ c.
1 c. raw cranberries,
   sliced
1 c. chopped nuts

Cream sugar and shortening. Add egg. Sift dry ingredients; add alternately with orange juice and water mixture. Fold in cranberries and nuts. Bake in a greased 9x5" loaf pan at 350° for 1 hour.

Marjorie Elliott

Lemon Loaf

Yield: 3 loaves

½ lb. butter
2½ c. sugar, divided
4 eggs
2 lemons, squeezed,
   rind grated
3 c. flour
2 t. baking powder
1 t. salt
1 c. milk
cream cheese, softened

Cream butter and 2 cups sugar together; add eggs one at a time, beating after each addition. Add lemon rind. Add sifted dry ingredients alternately with milk. Turn into 3 8x4" loaf pans; bake at 350° for 45-60 minutes. Place on wire racks covered with waxed paper. Combine remaining sugar with juice of lemons; drizzle over loaves; cool. To serve, slice thinly, spread with cream cheese and lightly toast. May be frozen.

Dode Macy (Mrs. Theodore)

Hiker's Health Bread

Yield: 1 loaf

2 c. unbleached flour
3 t. baking powder
1 t. salt
¼ c. dry milk
¼ c. wheat germ
1 c. all-bran cereal
½ c. honey
½ c. mashed banana
½ c. applesauce
½ c. vegetable oil
½ c. milk
2 beaten eggs
¼ c. raisins
¼ c. pitted chopped
   prunes
¼ c. chopped dates
¼ c. chopped nuts

Combine first six ingredients in large mixing bowl. In second bowl, stir remaining ingredients together; add to dry ingredients. Pour batter into a well greased 9x5" loaf pan. Bake 1 hour at 350° until pick inserted in middle comes out dry. (Nutritious with cream cheese.)

Pat Habig (Mrs. Franklin)

Orange-Date-Nut Bread

Yield: 1 loaf

1 orange, squeezed
1 c. chopped dates
1 t. baking soda
2 T. shortening
¾ c. sugar
1 t. vanilla
1 egg, beaten
2 c. flour
1 t. baking powder
salt
½ c. chopped nuts

Combine orange juice with enough boiling water to make 1 cup. Grate rind and add to dates. Add soda, shortening, sugar, vanilla and egg. Mix well. Sift flour with baking powder and salt. Combine two mixtures; add nuts. Turn into ungreased 9x5" loaf pan. Bake at 350° for 45 minutes.

Eleanor Pappky (Mrs. Herbert)

Pears and Cheese Quick Bread

Yield: 1 loaf

1 pkg. nut or date Quick
   Bread Mix
¾ c. finely diced canned
   pears, well drained
½ c. pear syrup
½ c. shredded cheddar
   cheese
1 egg

Combine all ingredients; stir 50-75 strokes until dry particles are moistened. Pour into generously greased 9x5" loaf pan. Bake at 350° for 55-65 minutes. Cool 15 minutes. Store in refrigerator.

Kay Plossl (Mrs. William)

Pineapple-Nut Bread

Yield: 1 loaf

2 c. flour
3 t. baking powder
1 t. salt
⅓ c. sugar
2 eggs, beaten
⅓ c. butter, melted
1 c. crushed pineapple, undrained
1 c. coarsely chopped walnuts or pecans

Sift flour, baking powder and salt together; add sugar. Combine eggs, butter and pineapple. Stir dry ingredients and nuts into egg mixture only enough to moisten. Bake at 350° in a greased 8x4" loaf pan for 1 hour.

Rose Donahue (Mrs. Gerald)

No-Knead Maple-Oatmeal Bread

Yield: 1 2 lb. loaf or 2 1 lbs. loaves

1¼ c. milk
4 T. butter
1 c. quick-cooking oats
1 pkg. dry yeast
¼ c. warm water (105°-115°)
⅓ c. maple syrup
1 egg
1½ t. salt
¾ c. whole wheat flour
2 c. unbleached flour
½ c. currants or raisins

Combine milk and butter; heat to boiling; pour over oats; cool to lukewarm. Dissolve yeast in water; stir in 1 teaspoon syrup; let stand undisturbed to "proof" until bubbly and doubled in volume. Add yeast mixture, remaining syrup, egg, salt, whole wheat flour and ¾ cup unbleached flour to oatmeal mixture. Beat with electric mixer at medium speed for 3 minutes. Stir in currants and remaining flour with a wooden spoon to make a soft dough.

Turn into 1 2 lb. or 2 1 lb. coffee cans (or 2 8x4" loaf pans) which have been greased and sprinkled on bottom and sides with additional oats. Let rise for 45 minutes in a warm place until doubled in bulk. Bake at 350° for 35 minutes for the 1 lb. cans and the loaf pans, 45-50 minutes for the 2 lb. can. If browning occurs too quickly, cover with foil. Cool on wire racks. Slice and toast.

Leanne Conte (Mrs. Frank)

Easter Bread

1 **yeast cake**
4 **t. sugar**
1 **c. lukewarm milk**
2¼ **c. flour**
⅓ **c. butter, melted**
2 **egg yolks**
1 **t. salt**
½ **c. currants**
grated rind of 1 lemon
¼ **c. chopped citron**
½ **c. seedless raisins**
2 **T. butter**
2 **T. bread crumbs**
4 **T. confectioners sugar**

Cover yeast with 1 teaspoon sugar and 1 tablespoon milk; let stand for 15 minutes; combine with flour. Add melted butter, egg yolks, salt and remaining sugar. Gradually mix in remaining milk. Fold in currants, lemon rind, citron and raisins. Place dough in an angel food or bundt pan which has been greased with the 2 tablespoons of butter and sprinkled with crumbs; let rise in a warm place for 1 hour. Bake at 350° for 45 minutes until inserted knife comes out clean; cool in pan for 10 minutes; dust with sugar when completely cooled.

Claire F. Cosgrove

Beer Bread

1 **12 oz. can beer**
3 **c. self-rising flour**
3 **T. sugar**
melted butter

Beat beer for 30 seconds. Combine all ingredients except butter; pour into a greased 9x5" loaf pan; brush top with butter. Bake at 375° for 45 minutes; cool. (Slices may be toasted, if desired.)

Trudy Haff (Mrs. Thomas)

Cheese Casserole Bread

Yield: 2 loaves

4¾ to 5½ c. flour,
  divided
3 T. sugar
1 T. salt
2 pkgs. dry yeast
1 c. milk
1 c. water
2 T. margarine
1½ c. grated sharp
  Cheddar or Swiss
  cheese
1 egg, at room
  temperature

Combine 1¾ cups flour, sugar, salt and yeast. Combine milk, water and margarine; cook over low heat until liquids are warm (margarine does not need to melt). Gradually add to dry ingredients; beat 2 minutes at medium speed of electric mixer, scraping bowl occasionally. Add cheese, egg and ½ cup flour, or enough flour to make a thick batter. Beat at high speed 2 minutes, scraping bowl occasionally. Stir in enough additional flour to make a stiff batter. Beat until well blended. Cover; let rise in a warm place for 40 minutes until doubled in bulk. Stir batter down; beat vigorously for ½ minute. Turn into 2 greased 1 quart casseroles. Bake at 375° for 40-50 minutes until done. Cool on wire racks.

Gerri Harter (Mrs. William)
Rosa Pudell

Dilly Casserole Bread

Yield: 1 loaf

1 pkg. dry yeast
¼ c. warm water
2 T. sugar, divided
1 c. cream-style cottage
  cheese
1 T. minced onion
2 t. dill seed
1 T. butter
1 t. salt
¼ t. baking soda
1 egg
2¼ c. instant flour
butter, melted

Dissolve yeast in water; add 1 tablespoon sugar. Combine remaining ingredients except melted butter; mix with yeast. Turn into a greased 8" casserole; let rise for 30-40 minutes. Bake at 350° for 40-50 minutes. Brush top with melted butter; sprinkle with salt.

Jeanne Brown (Mrs. Douglas)

Jalapeño Corn Bread

Yield: 3 loaves

2½ c. yellow cornmeal
1 c. stone-ground wholewheat flour
1 T. honey
1 T. salt (optional)
4 t. baking powder
1 t. baking soda
3 eggs, beaten at room temperature
½ c. buttermilk at room temperature
½ c. oil
1 17 oz. can creamed corn
6 jalapeño chili peppers seeded, chopped
2½ c. grated Cheddar cheese
1 large onion, grated

Combine first 6 ingredients. Combine eggs, milk and oil; add to cornmeal mixture. Add remaining ingredients, mixing well after each addition. Turn into 3 greased 8x4" loaf pans. Bake at 425° for 35-40 minutes; let stand in pans 10-15 minutes, then turn out on wire racks to cool.

Nancy Babcock

Mushroom Bread

Yield: 2 loaves

½ lb. fresh mushrooms, finely chopped
½ c. finely chopped onions
¼ c. margarine, divided
2 c. milk, scalded
3 T. molasses
4 t. salt
½ t. pepper
2 pkgs. dry yeast
½ c. warm water
1 egg
1½ c. wheat germ
8 c. flour, divided
butter, melted

Sauté onions and mushrooms in 2 tablespoons margarine until liquid has been absorbed; cool. Combine milk, remaining margarine, molasses, salt and pepper; cool. Sprinkle yeast over water; stir until dissolved; add to milk mixture. Add mushrooms, onions, egg, wheat germ and 2 cups flour, beating until smooth. Mix in remaining flour to form a stiff dough; knead 8 minutes until smooth and elastic. Turn into a greased bowl; cover, let rise until doubled in bulk. Divide dough in half; roll each to a 14x9" rectangle; fold to fit into 2 greased 9x5" loaf pans. Cover; let rise until double in bulk. Brush tops with butter; sprinkle lightly with salt. Bake at 400° for 45 minutes; cool on wire racks.

Linda Herm

Poppy Seed-Onion Bread

Yield: 1 loaf

1 pkg. dry yeast
¼ c. warm water
4½ c. flour, divided
¾ c. butter, melted, divided
1 c. warm milk
¼ c. sugar
2 t. salt, divided
1 egg
1 c. finely chopped onion
3 T. poppy seeds

Dissolve yeast in water; add 2 cups flour, ½ cup butter, milk, sugar, 1¾ teaspoons salt and egg; beat at medium speed for 2 minutes. Stir in remaining flour to make a stiff dough. Knead on lightly floured surface for 8-10 minutes until smooth and elastic. Place in greased bowl; invert to grease top; cover, let rise for 1-2 hours in warm place until doubled in bulk. Punch down dough; roll to a 20x8" rectangle on lightly floured surface; cut in half, forming 2 20x4" rectangles. Combine onion, poppy seeds and remaining butter and salt; spread on dough to within ½" of edges. Fold long sides together to form long "rope"; seal seams. Twist "ropes" together; form into a ring on lightly greased baking sheet, pinching together to seal. Cover; let rise for 1 hour until doubled in bulk. Brush with additional beaten egg; sprinkle with additional poppy seeds and chopped onion, if desired. Bake at 350° for 40 minutes until bread sounds hollow when tapped; cool on wire rack.

Eleanor Pappky (Mrs. Herbert)

Sausage Bread

Yield: 1 roll

1 lb. homemade or frozen bread dough
1 lb. sausage, cooked and drained
4 large onions, chopped, sauteed and drained
½ lb. mozzarella cheese, grated
oil
paprika

Roll dough into an 11x7" rectangle. Combine sausage, onions and cheese; spread on dough leaving half-inch margins. Roll up, starting at long end; seal seams with a little water. Place on a greased cookie sheet, seam side down. Brush with oil and sprinkle with paprika. Bake at 375° for 25 minutes.

Lucy Buonopane (Mrs. Mario)

Swedish Bread

Yield: 1 loaf

¼ c. honey
1 T. butter
1 t. instant ground
    coffee
1 t. fennel seeds
1 t. salt
1 c. milk, scalded
grated rind of 1 orange
3 T. sugar
1 pkg. dry yeast
½ t. ground cloves
1 c. rye flour
3¼ c. white flour

Combine first 5 ingredients; add scalded milk; cool. Add rind, sugar and yeast. Mix in cloves, rye flour and 1¼ cups white flour until dough is smooth; cover, let rise until doubled in bulk. Knead in remaining white flour; turn into a greased 9x5″ loaf pan; let rise until doubled in bulk. Bake at 350° for 45 minutes.

Rosa Pudell

Zucchini Bread

Yield: 2 loaves

3 eggs, beaten
2 c. sugar
1 c. oil
2 c. grated, peeled
    zucchini; hand-
    squeezed dry
½ t. vanilla
3 c. flour
2-3 t. cinnamon
1 t. salt
1 t. baking soda
1 t. baking powder
½ c. chopped nuts

Combine eggs, sugar, oil, zucchini and vanilla; stir in sifted dry ingredients; fold in nuts. Turn into 2 greased 9x5x3″ loaf pans; bake at 325° for 1 hour; cool in pans for 10 minutes; cool on wire racks. May be frozen.

Alicia Branch (Mrs. Elmer)
Pat Guinivan (Mrs. Thomas)
Ann Jamison (Mrs. R. Barnett, Jr.)
Lucille Mayer (Mrs. John)
Betty Miles (Mrs. Martin)
Marian Stuart (Mrs. Russell)

Everything Bread

Yield: 3 loaves

3 c. warm milk
3 t. salt
4 T. honey
1 pkg. dry yeast
9 c. flour, divided
½ c. quick oats
½ c. all-bran cereal
½ c. wheat germ
2 eggs, beaten
4 T. butter, melted

Combine milk, salt and honey; cool. Stir in 1 cup flour mixed with yeast, oats, all-bran and wheat germ. Stir in eggs, 2 cups of the flour, and butter. Add remaining flour (dough will be very stiff). Cover, let rise for 1 hour until double in bulk. Stir down; let stand for 15 minutes. Turn into 3 greased 9x5″ loaf pans; cover, let rise for 1 hour. Bake at 425° for 25 minutes.

Eleanor Flynn

Swedish Rye Bread

Yield: 2 loaves

2 c. warm water
½ c. brown sugar, packed
3 T. molasses
1 pkg. dry yeast
2 c. rye flour (not stone ground)
1 t. salt
1 t. caraway seeds
1 t. anise seeds
1 T. shortening, melted
3½ c. white flour

Warm a large bowl with hot water, then empty. Mix water, sugar and molasses in the warmed bowl; cool to lukewarm; add yeast, let stand for 20 minutes until bubbles form on top. Add rye flour; mix until most of the lumps are gone; let stand for 20-25 minutes until dough becomes sponge-like. Add salt, caraway seeds, anise seeds and shortening. Add white flour; mix well. Turn onto a floured surface; knead for 8-10 minutes. Place in a greased bowl; invert to grease top; cover, let rise for 1 hour in a warm place until doubled in bulk. Punch dough down; divide in half; let stand for 10 minutes. Shape into loaves in 2 greased 9x5" loaf pans. Brush tops with additional melted shortening. Let rise for 45-60 minutes until doubled in bulk. Bake at 350° for 45 minutes. Remove from pans immediately; brush tops with butter; cool.

Gerri Harter (Mrs. William)

No-Knead Whole Wheat Bread

Yield: 2 loaves

3 pkgs. dry yeast
4 c. lukewarm water
5 T. honey, divided
2 eggs, beaten
4 t. salt
½ c. bran
8 c. whole wheat flour, divided
raisins (optional)

Dissolve yeast in 1 cup water with 1 tablespoon honey. Combine eggs, salt, bran, remaining water and honey and 4 cups flour; beat with wooden spoon. Add yeast and remaining flour (dough will be sticky). Add raisins if desired. Spoon into 2 greased 9x5" loaf pans; let rise in a warm place for 1 hour, covered with towels until height exceeds pans. Bake at 400° for 50-60 minutes; cool in pans for 10 minutes. (May be frozen. For a less coarse dough, 2 cups white flour may be substituted for 2 cups of whole wheat flour.)

Barbara Brown (Mrs. Edward)

Macaroon Muffins

Yield: 24 muffins

1⅓ c. sugar, divided
¾ c. flour
½ t. baking powder
½ t. salt
6 egg whites
½ t. cream of tartar
½ t. vanilla
½ t. almond extract
3½ oz. sweetened
   coconut
almonds, sliced

Combine 1 cup of the sugar, flour, baking powder and salt. Beat egg whites with cream of tartar at low speed until foamy. Add remaining sugar; beat at high speed until stiff and glossy; add vanilla and almond extract. Fold flour mixture and coconut into egg whites. Turn into 2 inch paper lined muffin cups. Place 3 almond slices on each; bake at 300° for 40-45 minutes until browned.

Mary Lou Emerson (Mrs. Fred)

Featherlight Hot Cakes

Serves 4-6

4 eggs
1 pt. sour cream
1 T. butter, melted
1 c. flour, rounded
¾ t. salt

Beat eggs until light, add sour cream and butter. Sift dry ingredients together; add gradually and gently to egg mixture. Cook on a greased 450° griddle.

Lee Cowell (Mrs. John)

Sour Dough Starter

1 c. milk
1 c. flour

Place milk in glass jar or crock (nothing metal); allow to stand at room temperature for 24 hours. Stir in flour. Leave uncovered in a warm place (80°) for 2-5 days, until it bubbles and sours. If it starts to dry out, stir in enough tepid water to bring back to original consistency. Once it has a good sour aroma and is full of bubbles it is ready to use. Try to maintain about 1½ cups starter. Each time you use part of your starter, replenish it with a mixture of equal amounts of tepid water and flour. Leave it at room temperature several hours or overnight until it again becomes full of bubbles. Cover and store it in the refrigerator.

Ollie Irwin (Mrs. Pawlakos-Verne)

Sour Dough Pancakes   Yield: 25 dollar size pancakes

1 1 c. sour dough
   starter
2 c. warm water
2½ c. flour
1 egg
2 T. oil
¼ c. evaporated milk
1 t. salt
1 t. baking soda
2 T. sugar

Night before, place starter in bowl. Add water and flour. Mix thoroughly. (Mixture will be thick and lumpy but it will thin down from fermenting and be lively by breakfast time.) Cover bowl; set in warm spot overnight for complete fermentation. Important: In the morning remove 1 cup of starter and keep in the refrigerator until next time. Add egg, oil and milk to remaining starter; beat thoroughly. Combine salt, soda and sugar until smooth. Sprinkle evenly over top of batter; fold in gently. This will cause a gentle foaming action. Allow batter to rest a few minutes, then fry on a hot, lightly greased griddle. If the pancakes do not brown rapidly and sizzle slightly as you drop each tablespoonful of batter on the griddle, it isn't hot enough. If batter seems too thick, it wasn't warm enough to ferment sufficiently during the night. It may be thinned with a little milk. Sour dough batter is fairly thin but lively.

If you wish to serve a number of people, always increase the amount of starter in proportion. Do this by making the basic batter a day or two in advance. You can double, triple, quadruple, ad infinitum. Sour dough pancakes can be kept warm in oven and still retain their consistency.

Ollie Irwin (Mrs. Pawlakos-Verne)

Cottage Pancakes   Yield: 12 pancakes

1 c. cottage cheese
6 eggs
1 c. buttermilk
¾ c. sifted flour
1 T. sugar
½ t. salt
¼ t. baking soda
¼ t. baking powder

Combine all ingredients, beating well. Cook as any other pancake on a hot griddle.

Cyndi McJames (Mrs. William)

Bernice Merritt's Dinner Rolls

Yield: 48 rolls

2 eggs, beaten
½ c. sugar
1 c. cooked mashed
   potatoes
1 c. warm milk
1 ¼ oz. pkg. yeast,
   dissolved in ½ c.
   warm water
4-6 c. flour
1 t. salt
½ c. butter

Combine eggs, sugar, potatoes and milk; mix in dissolved yeast. Add 2½-3 cups flour gradually. Dough should be just thick enough to drop in blobs from a spoon. Cover, let rise 2½ hours. Add salt, butter and remaining flour. Dough should be less stiff than bread dough. At this point, dough can be refrigerated overnight.

Knead until smooth; let rise 2 hours. Divide dough into 4 parts; roll each into a 17″ circle. Cut each into 12 wedges; roll each wedge, starting from wide edge, to form crescent roll. Let rise 1½ hours. Bake 20 minutes at 350°.

Jean Anne Casey (Mrs. H. Craig)

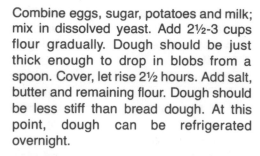

Buttery Croissants

Yield: 32 rolls

1 pkg. dry yeast
1 c. warm water
¾ c. evaporated milk
1½ t. salt
⅓ c. sugar
1 egg
5 c. flour, divided
¼ c. butter, melted,
   cooled
1 c. butter, unmelted
   egg glaze (1 egg beaten
   with 1 T. water)

Soften yeast in water; add milk, salt, sugar, egg and 1 cup flour; beat until smooth; add melted butter. Cut unmelted butter into remaining flour until dough resembles size of kidney beans; stir into yeast mixture until flour is moistened (do not overbeat as butter must remain kidney bean size). Chill for 4 hours. Divide dough into 4 parts; roll each into a 17″ circle; cut each into 8 wedges; roll from wide side to point and curve into crescent forms. Let rise for 2 hours at room temperature under a towel. Brush with egg glaze. Bake at 325° for 35 minutes.

Emma Horne (Mrs. James)

Hearty Wheat Rolls

Yield: 16 rolls

1 pkg. hot roll mix
1 c. warm water (105°-115°)
1 c. Farina or other wheat cereal, uncooked
¼ c. instant non-fat dry milk
3 T.honey
1 egg

Dissolve yeast from mix package in water; add cereal, dry milk, honey and egg; blend in flour from mix package. Cover, let rise for 45-60 minutes until doubled in bulk. Toss dough on well-floured surface until stickiness disappears; divide into 16 portions; shape into balls. Place in a greased 13x9″ baking pan; cover, let rise for 30-45 minutes until doubled in bulk. Bake at 350° for 20-30 minutes until golden brown.

Kay Plossl (Mrs. William)

English Muffins

Yield: 10-12 muffins

1 c. warm water
1 pkg. active dry yeast
1 t. sugar
2 t. salt
¼ c. soft shortening
3 c. sifted flour
cornmeal

Measure water into mixing bowl. Add yeast, stirring to dissolve. Stir in remaining ingredients. Mix until well blended and dough is soft. Roll out ¼ inch thick on floured board. Cut into ten-twelve 3½ inch circles. Place on cornmeal sprinkled baking sheet. Sprinkle muffins with cornmeal. Let rise in warm place, 85°, until double, about 1 hour. Bake on medium hot ungreased griddle or grill baker 7 minutes on each side. Split cooled muffins. Toast, butter and serve warm.

Linda Herm

Popovers

Yield: 8 popovers

1 c. flour, sifted
½ t. salt
2 eggs
1 c. milk
1 T. butter, melted

Sift flour into bowl. Add salt, eggs, milk and butter. Beat until mixture is smooth. Fill greased muffin tins two thirds full. Bake at 400° for 40 minutes until well puffed and golden. Pierce during last 5 minutes to allow steam to escape.

June McCann (Mrs. John)

Cakes, Cookies, Pies

Almond Cream Cake

Serves 8-10

1 c. heavy cream
2 eggs
¼ t. almond extract
1½ c. flour
1 c. sugar
2 t. baking powder
⅛ t. salt

Topping:
2 T. butter
⅓ c. sugar
1 T. flour
¼ c. blanched slivered
   almonds
heavy cream
almond extract

Reserve 1 tablespoon of the cream. Beat cream until soft peaks form. Add eggs one at a time, beating well after each addition. Stir in almond extract. Sift 1½ cups of the flour, sugar, baking powder and salt together; stir into cream mixture only until blended. Bake in a greased and floured 10″ spring form pan at 350° for 45 minutes until lightly browned on top and inserted toothpick comes out clean.

Topping: Combine butter, sugar, flour, almonds and reserved cream over low heat until blended; pour over cake. Bake at 350° for 10 minutes; cool. Garnish with additional heavy cream whipped with additional almond extract.

Ann Low (Mrs. Calvin)

German Apple Cake

Serves 10-12

4 eggs
2½ t. vanilla
⅓ c. orange juice
1 c. oil
2 c. sugar
3 c. flour
3 t. baking powder
5-6 apples
cinnamon-sugar mixture

Combine all ingredients except apples with mixer on low speed; beat for 10 minutes at medium speed. Pour ⅓ of the batter into a greased and floured 12-cup tube or bundt pan. Arrange half of the apples over batter; sprinkle with cinnamon-sugar. Repeat layers, ending with batter. Bake at 350° for 1 hour or more.

Doris Calvert (Mrs. William)

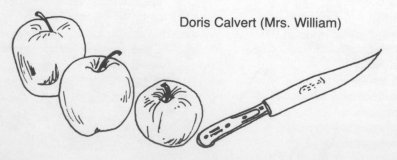

Stone Fence Applesauce Cake

Serves 10-12

¾ c. butter
1 c. sugar
1½ c. brown sugar,
    firmly packed
2 eggs
3 c. flour, unsifted
1½ c. whole wheat flour,
    unsifted
3 t. baking soda
1½ t. cinnamon
1½ t. nutmeg
1½ t. allspice
2¼ c. applesauce
¾ c. shredded carrots
1½ c. broken walnuts
1½ c. raisins
confectioners sugar

Cream butter; gradually beat in sugar; beat in eggs. Combine flours, baking soda and spices; add to egg mixture alternately with applesauce and carrots. Fold in walnuts and raisins. Bake in a greased and floured 9″ bundt pan at 350° for 1¼-1½ hours until browned and firm. Cool in pan for 5 minutes. Cool thoroughly on wire rack. Dust with confectioners sugar.

Fran Schnell (Mrs. William)

Blueberry Tea Cake

Serves 6-8

2 T. butter
1 c. sugar
2 eggs, separated
1½ c. flour
⅓ c. milk
1½ c. fresh blueberries,
    lightly floured
confectioners sugar

Cream butter and sugar; add beaten egg yolks. Add flour alternately with milk. Fold in stiffly beaten egg whites. Pour ½ of the batter into a greased 11¼x7¼″ pan or 9″ pie plate. Cover with blueberries; top with remaining batter. Bake at 350° for 35 minutes. Sprinkle with confectioners sugar.

Sheila Duetsch (Mrs. Bernard)

Cupcake Brownies

Yield: 12 cupcakes

½ c. butter
⅞ c. sugar
2 eggs
2 oz. semi-sweet
    chocolate, melted
⅝ c. flour
1 t. vanilla
¾ c. coarsely chopped
    pecans
12 chocolate-covered
    peppermints

Cream butter and sugar together. Beat in eggs. Stir in chocolate. Fold in flour, vanilla and nuts. Fill 12 muffin cups lined with paper liners ⅔ full. Bake at 325° for 35 minutes. Before removing from oven, place 1 peppermint candy on each; let soften, then swirl just enough to make a marbelized topping. Cool.

Claire Hadden (Mrs. William)

Tropical Carrot Cake

Serves 12

2 c. sugar
1½ c. oil
3 eggs
2 c. flour
1 t. baking soda
2 t. cinnamon
1 t. salt
2 c. finely grated carrots
1 c. drained crushed
   pineapple
1 c. coconut
1 c. chopped walnuts
1 t. vanilla

Frosting:
½ c. butter, softened
1 8 oz. pkg. cream
   cheese
1 1 lb. box
   confectioners sugar
1 T. instant chocolate
   (optional)
1 t. vanilla
coconut

Beat sugar, oil and eggs together with mixer; gradually add sifted dry ingredients. Fold in carrots, pineapple, coconut, walnuts and vanilla. Bake in a greased and floured 13x9″ pan at 350° for 1 hour; cool. Cream butter, cream cheese and confectioners sugar together. Add chocolate, vanilla and additional coconut; spread frosting on cake.

Mary Ann Crosby
Helene Herm (Mrs. Herbert)

Chocolate Angel Cake

Serves 12

1 10″ angel food cake
1½ pts. heavy cream
1½ c. confectioners
   sugar
¾ c. powdered cocoa
¼ t. salt
sliced almonds or 2-3
   crushed Heath bars

Invert cake on waxed paper; cut a 1″ slice off top of cake. With fingers, curved knife or spoon, hollow out a "canal" around center of cake to within 1″ of the bottom. In a chilled bowl, combine cream, sugar, cocoa and salt. Beat until stiff. Fill canal with ⅓ of whipped cream mixture. Replace top slice of cake; spread entire cake with remaining filling. Garnish with almonds. Chill.

Lee Moore (Mrs. Robert)

Santa Barbara Chocolate Chip Cake

Serves 12

2 c. cake flour, sifted
1¾ c. sugar
3 t. baking powder
1 t. salt
½ c. oil
7 eggs, separated
¾ c. cold water
2 t. vanilla
½ t. cream of tartar
3 oz. unsweetened chocolate, coarsely grated
1 lb. confectioners sugar
5-7 T. evaporated milk
3 oz. unsweetened chocolate, melted
¼ lb. butter, creamed

Combine flour, sugar, baking powder and salt in bowl. Make a well in center; add oil, unbeaten egg yolks, water and vanilla. Beat with spoon until smooth. Add cream of tartar to egg whites; beat until stiff peaks form. Pour egg yolk mixture gradually over whites, folding gently until just blended. Fold in chocolate. Bake in a 10" tube pan at 325° for 55 minutes, then at 350° for 10-15 minutes. Invert immediately, tube resting over neck of bottle; cool. Add sugar, milk and chocolate alternately to the butter; add additional milk if necessary for spreadable consistency.

Pat Guinivan (Mrs. Thomas)

Chocolate Peppermint Cake

Serves 8

¼ c. shortening
1 c. sugar
2 oz. unsweetened chocolate, melted
2 egg yolks
1 c. buttermilk
1½ c. flour
1 t. baking soda
salt
1 t. vanilla
3 T. water
3 drops peppermint oil
1 t. butter

Icing:
2 egg whites
1½ c. sugar
3 T. water
3 drops peppermint oil
1 oz. unsweetened chocolate
1 t. butter

Cream shortening and sugar together; add chocolate and slightly beaten egg yolks. Beat in milk, flour, baking soda, salt and vanilla. Bake in 2 greased 8" pans at 375° for 25 minutes; cool on wire racks.

Icing: Over hot water beat egg whites with remaining sugar and water; beat in oil until firm peaks form. Spread icing on cake. Heat remaining chocolate and butter together; drizzle over top of cake.

Marie Dreger (Mrs. E.E.)

Cranberry Swirl

Serves 10-12

½ c. unsalted butter
1 c. sugar
2 eggs
2 c. flour
1 t. baking powder
1 t. baking soda
1 c. sour cream or
   yogurt
1 t. almond extract
1 8 oz. can whole
   cranberry sauce
½ c. chopped nuts

Glaze:
¾ c. confectioners sugar
1-2 T. water
½ t. almond extract

Cream butter and sugar together; add eggs one at a time. Combine flour, baking powder and baking soda; add to egg mixture alternately with sour cream, ending with dry ingredients. Stir in almond extract. Spread ½ of the batter in a greased and floured 10″ bundt or tube pan. Spread with ½ of the cranberry sauce. Repeat layers. Sprinkle with nuts. Bake at 350° for 50-60 minutes; cool in pan. Combine confectioners sugar, water and extract. Drizzle glaze over cake.

Sharon Remlinger (Mrs. Donald)

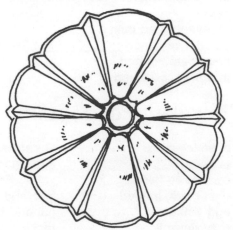

Date-Oatmeal Cake

Serves 8

1 c. boiling water
2 c. non-instant rolled
   oats
¾ c. butter
2 c. brown sugar
2 eggs
1½ c. chopped dates
1 c. chopped nuts
½ c. flour
1 t. baking soda
1 t. cinnamon

Pour water over oats; cool. Combine butter, sugar and eggs in food mixer; mix in dates and nuts. Stir in flour, baking soda, cinnamon and oats mixture. Spread into a 9″ square pan; bake at 350° for 45 minutes; cool; cut into squares.

Patricia Ellis (Mrs. Roy)

Holiday Cake

Serves 24

- 1¼ c. Cointreau
- ¾ c. finely chopped dried apricots
- ¾ c. coarsely chopped golden raisins
- ¾ c. finely chopped candied pineapple
- ½ c. finely chopped blanched almonds
- 12 large navel oranges
- 2 c. sifted flour
- ½ t. baking powder
- ½ t. salt
- ¼ t. mace
- 1 c. butter
- 1 c. sugar
- 5 eggs
- 1 t. grated lemon rind

Combine ½ cup Cointreau with apricots, raisins, pineapple and almonds; let stand at least 4 hours, stirring occasionally. Squeeze enough oranges to make ¾ cup juice. Remove pulp and membrane from all orange halves; place each shell on circle of foil just large enough to wrap around it. Place on cookie sheets. Sift pre-sifted flour, baking powder, salt and mace together. Cream butter and sugar; add eggs one at a time beating after each addition. Add flour mixture, beating until blended with mixer on low speed. Fold in lemon rind and fruit mixture. Fill orange shells half full with batter; bake at 350° for 35 minutes until cakes are done; place on wire racks. While cakes are still warm, baste each with ½ tablespoon combined reserved orange juice and remaining Cointreau. Store for 2-3 days, wrapped in foil, before serving. May also be baked in a tube pan.

Madeleine Schulhoff (Mrs. Joseph)

Norwegian Gold Cake

Serves 8-10

- 1 c. butter, softened
- 1⅓ c. flour
- 5 eggs
- 1⅓ c. sugar
- 1½ t. baking powder
- ½ t. salt
- 1 t. vanilla
- Amaretto

Combine butter and flour; beat in eggs one at a time. Add sugar, baking powder, salt, and vanilla; beat for 2 minutes with mixer. Bake in greased and floured 9″ bundt pan at 325° for 1 hour. Pour Amaretto over individual servings.

Dee Bull (Mrs. Calvin)

Pumpkin Cake Roll

Serves 8

3 eggs
1 c. sugar
⅔ c. pumpkin
1 t. lemon juice
¾ c. flour
1 t. baking powder
2 t. cinnamon
1 t. ginger
½ t. salt
½ t. nutmeg
1 c. finely chopped
  walnuts
1 c. confectioners sugar
  plus extra for dusting

Filling:
2 3 oz. pkgs. cream
  cheese
4 T. butter
½ t. vanilla

Beat eggs for 5 minutes with mixer on high speed. Gradually beat in sugar. Stir in pumpkin and lemon juice. Combine flour, baking powder, ginger, salt and nutmeg; fold into pumpkin mixture. Spread in a greased and floured 15x10″ jelly roll pan; top with walnuts; bake at 375° for 15 minutes. Turn out on towel sprinkled with confectioners sugar; starting at narrow end, roll cake and towel together; cool; unroll.

Filling: Combine cheese, butter and vanilla. Spread over cake; roll; chill.

Samantha Potts

Prune Cake

Serves 10-12

1 c. oil
2 c. sugar
3 eggs
3 c. sifted flour
1 t. salt
1 t. baking soda
1 t. cinnamon
1 t. cloves
1 t. nutmeg
1 c. buttermilk
1 c. cooked mashed
  prunes
½ c. chopped nuts

Glaze:
2 T. butter
½ c. buttermilk
1 c. sugar
½ t. baking soda

Cream oil and sugar together; add eggs. Combine flour, salt, baking soda and spices. Add to oil mixture alternately with 1 cup of the buttermilk; add prunes and nuts. Bake in a greased 10″ tube pan at 300° for 1 hour.

Glaze: Combine butter, remaining buttermilk, sugar and baking soda; boil for 1-2 minutes; pour over warm cake, inserting fork into cake to allow some of the glaze to be absorbed.

Susan Johnson (Mrs. Roger)

Easy Pound Cake

½ lb. butter, softened
1⅔ c. sugar
5 eggs
2 c. sifted flour (sift
   before measuring)

Cream butter and sugar. Add eggs. Add flour; beat with mixer for 4-5 minutes or by hand to a creamy consistency. Bake in a greased and floured 9x5″ or 13x4½″ loaf pan at 325° for 45-60 minutes until inserted toothpick comes out clean.

Ruth Miller (Mrs. James)

Autumn Pound Cake

Serves 12

2½ c. sifted flour
1 t. baking powder
½ t. baking soda
2 t. cinnamon
½ t. salt
½ c. butter, softened
1½ c. sugar
3 eggs
1 c. yogurt
½ c. pumpkin
1 c. chopped walnuts

Frosting:
1 3 oz. pkg. cream
   cheese, softened
½ t. vanilla
2 c. sifted confectioners
   sugar
whole walnuts

Combine first 5 ingredients. Beat butter until fluffy with mixer at medium speed; gradually beat in sugar. Add eggs one at a time, beating after each addition. At low speed, beat in ½ of the flour mixture, yogurt and pumpkin. Add remaining flour mixture, beating until smooth. Stir in walnuts. Pour into greased and floured 9″ tube pan. Bake at 325° for 55-60 minutes until inserted toothpick comes out clean. Cool in pan on wire rack for 10 minutes. Unmold onto rack and cool completely.

Frosting: Beat cream cheese and vanilla at low speed until fluffy; gradually beat in confectioners sugar; spread on top of cake. Garnish with whole walnuts.

Joanne Keith (Mrs. James)

Quick Orange Cake

Serves 6

½ c. melted margarine
1 c. sugar
2 eggs
¾ c. orange juice
2 c. flour
4 t. baking powder
½ t. salt
rind of 1 large orange
3 t. sugar

Melt shortening. Add sugar to pan; beat 2 minutes. Add eggs, one at a time, beating after each. Add sifted dry ingredients, by hand, alternately with orange juice, starting and ending with flour. Work as quickly as possible. Pour batter into 8x8″ pan. Sprinkle with orange rind and sugar. Bake at 350° for 50 minutes.

Ann Harrison (Mrs. Thomas)

Sauerkraut Cake

12 T. butter, divided
1½ c. sugar
3 eggs
2 t. vanilla, divided
2 c. flour
1 t. baking powder
1 t. baking soda
¼ t. salt
½ c. powdered cocoa
1 c. water
1 8 oz. can sauerkraut,
   drained, rinsed, finely
   chopped
Frosting:

1 6 oz. pkg. semi-sweet
   chocolate bits
½ c. sour cream
confectioners sugar

Beat 8 tablespoons of the butter and sugar together. Add eggs one at a time, beating after each addition; add 1 teaspoon of the vanilla. Sift dry ingredients together. Add to egg mixture alternately with water, beating after each addition; stir in sauerkraut. Bake in a greased and floured 13x9″ pan at 350° for 35-40 minutes; cool in pan.

Frosting: Melt chocolate and remaining butter together; blend in sour cream and remaining vanilla. Beat in enough confectioners sugar for spreading consistency; spread on cake.

Faye Kennedy (Mrs. Richard)

Sour Cream Cake

¼ lb. butter
1 c. sugar
2 eggs
2 c. flour
1 t. baking powder
1 t. baking soda
1 c. sour cream
1 t. vanilla
½ c. semi-sweet
   chocolate bits or
   golden raisins
½ c. brown sugar, firmly
   packed
½ c. coarsely chopped
   nuts
1 t. cinnamon
thin chocolate mint
   wafers (optional)

Cream butter and sugar; beat in eggs until fluffy. Sift flour, baking powder and baking soda together; add alternately with sour cream. Stir in vanilla and chocolate chips or raisins. Spoon into a greased and floured 10″ tube pan. Combine brown sugar, nuts and cinnamon; press evenly into the surface of the batter. Bake at 350° for 45-50 minutes. Invert on rack and remove cake from pan. Invert at once on another rack to cool with the top up. Decorate with mint wafers.

Edna Vogel (Mrs. Nathan)

Bourbon-Walnut Cake

Serves 12-16

2 c. finely chopped
   walnuts
1 c. bourbon, divided
3½ c. sifted flour
1½ t. baking powder
½ t. salt
¼ t. nutmeg
¼ t. cinnamon
¼ t. ground cloves
2 c. butter, softened
2½ c. sugar
8 eggs, beaten
1 t. vanilla

Marinate walnuts in ½ cup bourbon. Sift dry ingredients and spices together. Cream butter and sugar until light. Add eggs and vanilla, beating at high speed, for 4 minutes until thick and fluffy. At low speed, gradually beat in flour mixture until just combined; stir in walnut-bourbon mixture. Bake in greased and floured 10″ tube pan at 350° for 70 minutes. Cool in pan on wire rack for 15 minutes; remove from pan; cool completely on wire rack. Soak a large piece of cheesecloth in remaining bourbon; wrap cake in cheesecloth, then in foil; seal in plastic bag. Refrigerate for several days.

Viola Krasny (Mrs. Jack)

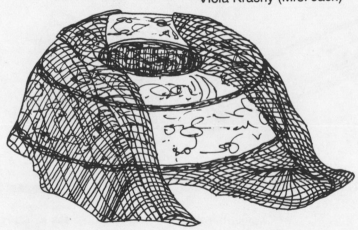

The Best Chocolate Icing

1 c. sugar
3 T. cornstarch
2 oz. unsweetened
   chocolate, broken into
   pieces
salt
1 c. boiling water
3 T. butter
1 t. vanilla

Combine sugar and cornstarch thoroughly. Add chocolate, salt and water; cook until thickened, stirring constantly. Add butter and vanilla. Spread on 8″ layer cake while hot.

Bella Neifeld (Mrs. Martin)

Apple Butter Buttons

Yield: 2 dozen

½ c. shortening,
  softened
1 c. sugar
2 eggs
2 T. sour cream
1 t. vanilla
2½ c. sifted flour
¼ t. baking soda
1½ t. baking powder
½ t. salt
apple butter

Mix shortening, sugar and eggs to-gether; stir in sour cream and vanilla. Combine dry ingredients; stir into egg mixture. Chill at least 1 hour. Roll dough on floured surface to ⅛ inch thickness. Cut rounds with a floured 2″ cookie cut-ter. Place ½ of the rounds on a lightly greased cookie sheet. Top each with a rounded teaspoonful of apple butter. Make four slits in centers of remaining rounds and place over filled rounds, pressing edges together with fork tines to seal. Bake at 400° for 8-10 minutes. A nice unusual cookie for apple butter fans.

Maryalice Marakas (Mrs. James)

Apples and Oats Cookies

Yield: 3 dozen

1½ c. oats
¾ c. flour
¾ c. whole wheat flour
¼ c. brown sugar, firmly
  packed
¼ c. sesame seeds
1½ t. baking powder
1½ t. cinnamon
¼ t. salt
1 c. unpeeled chopped
  apples
½ c. honey
½ c. oil
1 egg, beaten
⅓ c. milk

Combine first 8 ingredients; stir in ap-ples. Combine honey, oil, egg and milk; mix into dry ingredients. Drop by tea-spoonfuls on ungreased baking sheet. Bake at 375° for 10-12 minutes. Cool on wire racks.

Carolyn Walters

Butter Pecan Turtle Cookies

Yield: 16-24 bars

2 c. flour
1½ c. brown sugar,
    firmly packed, divided
½ + ⅔ c. butter,
    softened
1 c. chopped pecans
1 c. milk chocolate
    chips

Mix flour, 1 cup of the brown sugar and ½ cup of the butter for 2-3 minutes with electric mixer at medium speed. Press into a greased 13x9" baking pan; sprinkle with pecans. Boil remaining sugar and butter over medium heat for 1 minute, stirring constantly; pour over pecans. Bake at 350° for 18-22 minutes until caramel is bubbly and crust is golden. Sprinkle with chocolate; let stand for 2-3 minutes until melted; swirl chocolate over surface. Cool; cut into bars.

Mary Lou Emerson (Mrs. Fred)

Christmas Casserole Cookies

Yield: 3 dozen

2 eggs, beaten
1 c. sugar
1 c. pitted dates,
    coarsely chopped
1 c. coconut
1 c. chopped nuts
1 T. rum or 1 t. vanilla
    and ¼ t. almond
    extract
sugar

Combine eggs and sugar, beating until light; mix in remaining ingredients. Bake in an ungreased 2 quart casserole at 350° for 30 minutes. While still hot, beat well with wooden spoon; cool. Form into balls; roll in sugar.

Doreen Iossa (Mrs. Frederick)

Chocolate Meringues

Yield: 4 dozen

3 egg whites
1 c. confectioners sugar
12 saltines, crushed
½ c. nuts, optional
7 oz. semi-sweet
    chocolate, melted
1 t. vanilla

Beat egg whites until stiff; add sugar a little at a time. Add nuts, cracker crumbs, chocolate and vanilla. Drop on paper lined cookie sheet. Bake at 350° for 8-10 minutes.

Mary E. Kemmerer (Mrs. John)

Date-Nut Pinwheels

Yield: 7-8 dozen

1 c. shortening
2 c. brown sugar, firmly
packed
3 eggs, beaten
4 c. flour
½ t. baking soda
¼ t. salt

Filling:
2¼ c. chopped dates
1 c. sugar
1 c. water
1 c. chopped walnuts

Cream shortening and brown sugar to-gether; mix in eggs slowly until creamy. Add flour, baking soda and salt. Chill for at least 4 hours. Divide into 4 parts. Roll each into a ¼" thick rectangle. Cook dates, sugar and water for 10 minutes on low heat; stir in nuts. Cool. Spread filling on dough; roll up jelly-roll fashion; wrap in waxed paper. Freeze for at least 2 hours until firm enough to slice ¼" thick. Bake on cookie sheets at 400° for 10-12 minutes.

Marcia Grunwald (Mrs. Richard)

Double Decker Date-Nut Cookies

Yield: 18 bars

Crust:
1¼ c. sifted flour
⅓ c. sugar
½ c. butter

Filling:
⅓ c. sugar
⅓ c. light brown sugar,
firmly packed
2 eggs
1 t. vanilla
2 T. flour
1 t. baking powder
½ t. salt
1 c. chopped walnuts
1 8 oz. pkg. dates,
chopped
confectioners sugar

Combine flour, sugar and butter with pastry blender until mixture resembles fine crumbs; press into bottom of a greased 8 or 9" square pan. Bake at 350° for 15-20 minutes until edges are lightly browned. Beat sugars, eggs and vanilla together. Sift flour with baking powder and salt; add to egg mixture. Stir in walnuts and dates; pour over pastry mixture. Bake at 350° for 20 minutes; cool in pan. Sprinkle with confectioners sugar. Cut into bars.

Helen Fromel (Mrs. Robert)

No-Bake Date-Nut Krunchies

Yield: 3-4 dozen

½ c. butter, melted
½ c. sugar
1 egg
1 t. vanilla
½ lb. dates, chopped
½ c. chopped nuts
2½ c. Rice Krispies
confectioners sugar

Beat butter, sugar and egg together; add dates. Cook, stirring constantly, until browned. Stir in vanilla, nuts and cereal. Cool. Roll into small balls and coat with confectioners sugar.

Julie Planck (Mrs. J. Kent)

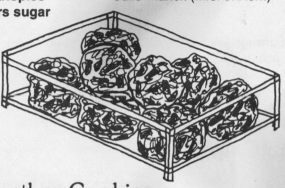

Grandmother Cookies

Yield: 4 dozen

24 plain graham crackers
¼ lb. butter
1 c. light brown sugar
1 c. chopped walnuts

Spread crackers on buttered cookies sheet that has a rim. Melt butter; add sugar; bring to boil. Boil moderately for 2 minutes. Add nuts; spread mixture over crackers. Bake at 350° for 10 minutes. Cookies will look soupy but will soon harden. Cut while warm into 48 pieces.

Edna VanSickle Budd (Mrs. Merritt)

Granny Cookies

Yield: 3 dozen

¾ c. shortening
1½ c. brown sugar
1 egg
¼ c. water
1 t. vanilla
1 c. whole wheat flour
1 t. salt
½ t. baking soda
2 c. granola
1 c. chocolate chips

Beat shortening and sugar together; add egg, water and vanilla. Sift dry ingredients together; stir into batter; add granola and chocolate chips. Drop by rounded teaspoonfuls on lightly greased cookie sheet, 2 inches apart. Bake at 400° for 10-12 minutes. Remove to wire rack immediately to cool.

Sally Shabaker (Mrs. Robert)

Orange Granola Cookies

Yield: 48

2 c. flour
2½ t. baking powder
1½ t. cinnamon
½ t. baking soda
½ t. salt
¼ t. ground cloves
½ c. butter, softened
½ c. sugar
1 egg
⅓ c. frozen orange juice
  concentrate
½ c. honey
1 c. raisins
1 c. uncooked oats
½ c. sunflower seed

Stir together dry ingredients. Cream butter and sugar until light. Beat in egg. Alternately stir in flour mixture, orange juice and honey until blended. Stir in raisins, oats and sunflower seeds. Drop by teaspoonfuls 2 inches apart on greased cookie sheet. Bake at 350° for 15-20 minutes.

Charlanne Lamberto (Mrs. Victor)

Kahluha Chip Cookies

Yield: 3 dozen

½ c. butter
1 egg
½ c. sifted sugar
¼ c. sifted brown sugar
1 T. Kahluha (or
  Creme de Cacao)
½ t. powdered coffee
  or 1 t. grated orange
  rind
1 c. sifted flour
½ t. baking soda
½ c. coarsely chopped
  nuts
1 c. coarsely chopped
  bittersweet chocolate

Beat butter and egg together until fluffy. Gradually stir in sugars; beat in liqueur and coffee; stir into egg mixture. Add combined flour and baking soda; stir in nuts and chocolate. Drop by teaspoonfuls on an ungreased cookie sheet. Bake at 375° for 8-10 minutes. Cool on wire racks.

Rosalyn Scheidlinger

Greek Christmas Cookies

Yield: 6 dozen

1 lb. whipped sweet
  butter, melted
7 T. water
7 T. + 1½ c.
  confectioners sugar
5 t. vanilla
4 c. flour
2 c. coarsley chopped
  walnuts

Beat butter, water, 7 tablespoons of the sugar and vanilla together. Beat in flour. Fold in walnuts. Drop by tablespoonfuls on ungreased cookie sheets. Bake at 350° for 25-30 minutes until lightly browned. While still warm, dip each cookie into sifted remaining sugar.

Steve Kostaras

Dark Herb Cookies

Yield: 3 dozen

½ c. butter
½ c. sugar
1 egg
½ c. molasses
2½ c. flour, sifted
2 t. soda
3 t. ginger
1 t. cinnamon
½ t. ground cloves
½ t. salt
⅓ c. hot strong coffee
2 T. anise seed
2 t. crushed coriander
  seed
2 c. confectioners
  sugar
1 t. vanilla
milk
nut halves

Cream butter and sugar together; beat in egg; stir in molasses. Sift flour and spices together; add alternately with coffee to creamed mixture. Stir in herb seeds. Drop by teaspoonfuls onto greased cookie sheet, 2 inches apart. Bake at 350° for 8-10 minutes. Cool. Frost with glaze of combined confectioners sugar, vanilla and enough milk for spreading consistency. Top each cookie with nut half.

Penny Peniston (Mrs. S.)

Melt-in-the-Mouth Cookies

Yield: 6-7 dozen

½ c. butter, softened
1 c. light brown sugar,
  firmly packed
1 egg
1 t. vanilla
¾ c. sifted flour
1 t. baking powder
½ t. salt
½ c. finely chopped nuts

Beat butter, sugar, egg and vanilla together until light and fluffy. Beat in sifted dry ingredients until smooth. Stir in nuts. Drop by level teaspoonfuls on ungreased cookie sheet. Bake at 400° for 5 minutes until lightly browned. Cool on wire racks.

Mary Ann Crosby

Mincemeat Cookies

Yield: 48

1 c. butter
1½ c. sugar
3 eggs
1 9 oz. pkg. mincemeat,
  crumbled
3¼ c. sifted flour
1 t. baking soda
½ t. salt

Cream butter and sugar until light and fluffy. Add eggs, one at a time, beating well. Beat in mincemeat. Add dry ingredients. Drop by tablespoonfuls onto ungreased cookie sheet 2 inches apart. Bake at 400° for 10 minutes.

Eleanor Mason

Oatmeal Party Cookies

Yield: 4½ dozen

1 c. butter, softened
1 c. sifted
   confectioners sugar
2 t. vanilla
½ t. salt
2 c. sifted flour
1 c. quick-cooking oats
1 6 oz. pkg. semisweet
   chocolate bits
¼ c. finely chopped
   walnuts

Cream butter, sugar, vanilla and salt together until light and fluffy; stir in flour and oats. Using about 2 teaspoonfuls for each, shape into 1 inch balls or 1½ inch logs. Bake on an ungreased cookie sheet at 325° for 20-25 minutes; cool on rack. Melt chocolate over hot water; dip tops of round cookies (or one end of each log) in chocolate; then in walnuts. Let set ovenight in a cool place.

Betty Breining (Mrs. C.M.)

Peanut Blossoms

Yield: 3 dozen

1 c. shortening
½ c. peanut butter
½ c. sugar
½ c. brown sugar
1 egg
1 t. vanilla
1¾ c. flour
1 t. baking soda
½ t. salt
semi-sweet chocolate
   bits

Combine shortening, peanut butter and sugars; stir in egg and vanilla. Add combined dry ingredients. Shape into balls; roll in additional sugar. Bake on an ungreased cookie sheet at 375° for 10 minutes. Press a semi-sweet chocolate bit in center of each cookie; bake for 2-5 minutes.

Eleanor Flynn

New Year's Sesame Balls

Yield: 3 dozen

1 c. shortening, melted
½ c. light brown sugar
1 T. water
1 t. vanilla
½ c. toasted sesame
   seed
2 c. flour, sifted

Combine shortening, sugar, water and vanilla. Toast sesame seeds by placing seeds in skillet; stir over medium heat until golden, about 1 minute. Do not use oil. Blend flour and sesame seeds into shortening mixture. Shape dough into ¾" balls. Bake on an ungreased sheet at 300° for 20 minutes until just golden. When cooled, roll in granulated sugar. Open Sesame the door to good fortune at midnight on New Year's Eve.

Penny Peniston

Sun's Up Cookies

Yield: 3 dozen

¾ c. margarine,
 softened
¾ c. brown sugar
¾ c. sugar
2 eggs
1 t. vanilla
1 c. coconut
1 c. whole wheat flakes
1 c. quick oats
2 c. whole wheat flour
½ t. salt
½ t. baking powder
½ t. baking soda
1 c. raisins

Beat margarine with sugars. Beat in eggs and vanilla. Gradually mix in remaining ingredients. Shape into 1½-2 inch balls. With palm of hand, flatten on greased cookie sheet. Bake at 350° for 12-15 minutes until lightly browned.

Penny Peniston (Mrs. S.)

Welsh Cookies

Yield: 40 cookies

4 c. flour
4 t. baking powder
1 t. salt (scant)
1 c. shortening
1¾ c. sugar
½ t. nutmeg
1½ c. raisins
2 eggs
½ c. milk
confectioners sugar

Sift flour, baking powder and salt together; work in shortening and sugar with a pastry blender. Add nutmeg and raisins; mix well. Make a well in center of batter; drop in eggs and milk; mix with a fork until crumbly. Refrigerate several hours or overnight. Roll out on a floured cloth; cut with a 2½ inch cookie cutter. Cook, as a pancake, on an ungreased griddle or in electric fry pan at 350° for 3 minutes until underside is shiny. Flip over and cook 3 minutes more. Dip completely in confectioners sugar and cool on a rack. Can be frozen or stored in a tin with a slice of fresh bread. (When ovens were not available in rural Wales, these tasty cookies were "baked" on a griddle.)

Dorothy Royer (Mrs. Robert)

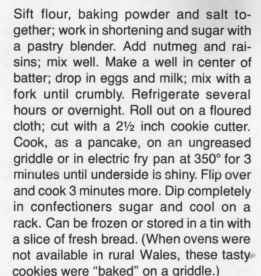

Lime Bars

2 c. flour
½ c. confectioners sugar
1 c. butter
4 eggs
2 c. sugar
salt
⅓ c. fresh lime juice
confectioners sugar

Combine flour and sugar; cut in butter. Press into 13x9" pan. Bake at 350° for 20-25 minutes until golden. Beat eggs at high speed until light. Gradually beat in sugar, salt and lime juice. Pour over hot crust. Bake 20-25 minutes longer until golden. Sprinkle at once with confectioners sugar. Cool; cut into bars.

The Committee

Honey Glow Bars

½ c. butter, softened
½ c. + 2 T.
  confectioners sugar
1 t. lemon extract
1½ c. flour
½ t. salt
2 T. milk
1 c. oatmeal
½ c. honey

Cream butter and ½ cup of the sugar together; add extract. Combine flour and salt; add alternately with milk to creamed mixture, beating well. Stir in oats. Press into a greased 11x7" baking pan. Make "wells" in dough with back of spoon; drizzle with honey. Bake at 325° for 25-30 minutes until honey is absorbed. Cool in pan on wire rack; cut into bars. Sprinkle with remaining sugar.

Charlanne Lamberto (Mrs. Victor)

Jam-Jams

2 c. oatmeal
1 c. flour
½ c. sugar
2 t. baking powder
½ t. salt
¾ c. shortening

Filling:
1 8 oz. pkg. dates or
  any combination of
  dates, figs, currants,
  raisins
½ c. sugar
½ t. vanilla
chopped nuts

Combine oatmeal, flour, sugar, baking powder and salt; cut in shortening. Press ½ of the mixture into bottom of a 9" square baking pan. Add enough cold water to dates to cover; add sugar. Cook until softened and thickened (add more water if necessary); chill. Add vanilla. Spread fruit filling on crust. Top with remaining crust, pressing lightly. Sprinkle with nuts if desired. Bake at 375° for 30 minutes until browned. Cool. Cut into squares.

Kay Dowd (Mrs. Russell)

Meringue Bars

Yield: 24-48 bars

1 c. butter, softened
½ c. sifted
  confectioners sugar
2 eggs, separated
1 c. fork-stirred
  unsifted flour
¾ c. currant jelly
½ c. sugar
¼ t. cinnamon
¾ c. finely chopped
  pecans

Cream butter and confectioners sugar together; beat in egg yolks; gradually beat in flour. Spread in bottom of an ungreased 13x9" baking pan. Bake at 350° for 10 minutes. Spread jelly on hot crust. Beat sugar, 2 tablespoons at a time, into stiffly beaten egg whites until glossy. Beat in cinnamon and fold in pecans. Drop by tablespoonfuls on jelly, spreading to cover jelly. Bake at 350° for 25 minutes. Cool in pan on wire rack.

Betty Ziegler (Mrs. John)

Apricot Bars

Yield: 3 dozen

1½ c. flour
1 t. baking powder
¼ t. salt
1½ c. quick cooking
  oatmeal
1 c. brown sugar
¾ c. butter
¾ c. apricot preserve

Combine flour, baking powder, salt, oatmeal, and brown sugar. Cut in butter. Put ⅔ of the crumb mixture into 8x8" pan. Spread with preserves. Cover with remaining crumb mixture. Bake at 375° for 25 minutes. Cool; cut into bars.

Mary Kay Reber (Mrs. George)

Oatmeal-Lemonade Bars

Yield: 36 bars

Crumb Mixture:
¾ c. butter, softened
1 c. brown sugar
1¾ c. flour
1 t. baking soda
1 t. salt
1¾ c. oats

Filling:
1 12 oz. pkg. dates,
  chopped
1 6 oz. can frozen
  lemonade, thawed
6 oz. water
¾ c. chopped walnuts
⅓ c. sugar
¼ c. flour
½ t. salt

Beat butter and sugar together until creamy; stir in flour, baking soda and salt; stir in oats; press ¼ of crumb mixture into bottom of a greased 13x9" baking pan.

Filling: Bring dates, lemonade and water to a boil; simmer for 15-20 minutes until thickened; stir in walnuts, sugar, remaining flour and salt; spread over crumb mixture; sprinkle with remaining crumbs. Bake at 400° for 25-30 minutes; cool; cut into bars.

Charlanne Lamberto (Mrs. Victor)

Lincoln Logs

Yield: 18-20 logs

2 c. graham cracker
  crumbs
1 c. semi-sweet
  chocolate mini-chips
1 14 oz. can condensed
  milk
1 t. vanilla
½ c. chopped nuts
confectioners sugar

Combine all ingredients except confectioners sugar. Bake in a greased and floured 8″ square pan at 350° for 20-30 minutes. Cool and cut into narrow bars. Roll in confectioners sugar.

Ruth Anspach
Ginny Militzer (Mrs. Kenneth)
Maisie Nelson (Mrs. Albert)

Scotcheroos

Yield: 60 squares

1 c. light corn syrup
1 c. sugar
1 c. peanut butter
6 c. Rice Krispies
1 12 oz. pkg. semi-sweet
  chocolate bits, melted

Combine syrup and sugar; bring to a boil. Add peanut butter and Rice Krispies. Spread into bottom of a greased 13x9″ pan. Spread with melted chocolate. Chill until chocolate is firm. Bring to room temperature to facilitate cutting into squares. (Easy, no-bake dessert)

Nancy Morrow (Mrs. David)

Zucchini Bars

Yield: 16 bars

¾ c. butter
½ c. brown sugar
½ c. sugar
2 eggs
1 t. vanilla
1¾ c. flour
1½ t. baking powder
2 c. peeled or unpeeled
  zucchini, shredded
1 c. coconut
¾ c. finely chopped
  walnuts

Cream butter until fluffy; beat in sugars. Beat in eggs one at a time; add vanilla. Stir in flour, baking powder, zucchini, coconut and walnuts. Bake in a greased 15x10″ baking pan at 350° for 40 minutes; cool. Melt butter; combine with confectioners sugar, milk, vanilla and cinnamon. Spread cake with glaze. Cut into bars.

Gini von Hoffmann (Mrs. Bernard)

Glaze:
1½ T. butter
1 c. confectioners sugar
2½ T. milk
½ t. cinnamon
1 t. vanilla

Apple Pie Normandie

Serves 6-8

1¼ c. sugar, divided
8 T. flour, divided
1 c. sour cream
1 egg, beaten
¼ t. salt
½ t. vanilla
2 c. apples, finely chopped
1 9″ pie shell, baked
1 t. cinnamon
4 T. butter

Combine ¾ cup sugar and 2 T. flour; add sour cream, egg, salt and vanilla; stir in apples; pour into pie shell; bake at 450° for 30 minutes until almost set. Combine remaining sugar and flour with cinnamon and butter until crumbly; sprinkle on pie; bake an additional 10 minutes.

Rose Donahue (Mrs. Gerald)
Anne Urban (Mrs. Robert)

Swedish Apple Pie

Serves 6-8

¼ c. shortening
¾ c. sugar, divided
2 eggs, separated
½ c. flour, sifted
½ t. baking powder
¼ t. salt
1 T. milk
1 t. vanilla
1 c. applesauce, chilled
heavy cream, whipped

Cream shortening and ¼ cup sugar; add egg yolks; stir in flour, baking powder, salt, milk and vanilla; turn into 8 or 9″ greased pie plate. Spread applesauce on top. Beat remaining sugar with egg whites until stiff; spread on top of applesauce; bake at 300° for 1 hour; chill; garnish with cream.

Helen Rossmeisl (Mrs. Herbert J., Jr.)

Chocolate Angel Pie

Serves 6-8

½ c. sugar
⅛ t. cream of tartar
2 egg whites, stiffly beaten (but not dry)
½ c. chopped walnuts or pecans
¾ c. semi-sweet chocolate bits, melted
3 T. hot water
1 t. vanilla
1 c. heavy cream, whipped

Sift sugar and cream of tartar together; add to egg whites, continuing to beat until smooth. Pour into a well greased 9″ pie plate, keeping center hollowed out to ¼″ thickness (do NOT spread meringue on rim of plate). Sprinkle with nuts. Bake at 275° for 1 hour. Cool completely.

Combine chocolate and water in double boiler; cook until thickened; cool slightly; add vanilla; fold in cream; turn into meringue shell. Chill at least 2-3 hours.

Peggy Chussler
Helen Rossmeisl (Mrs. Herbert J., Jr.)

199

Black Bottom Peppermint Pie

Serves 6-8

2 squares unsweetened
   chocolate
2 T. butter
½ c. sugar
1 T. cornstarch
salt
1 c. milk
½ t. vanilla
1 9″ pie shell, baked
3 pts. peppermint stick
   ice cream
chopped nuts (optional)

Melt chocolate and butter over low heat; stir in sugar, cornstarch and salt; gradually add milk; cook over medium heat, stirring constantly, until thickened; cook an additional 2 minutes; add vanilla. Pour ½ cup of mixture into pie shell, coating bottom and sides; freeze. Spoon half of the ice cream on top; drizzle with ½ of the remaining chocolate mixture; freeze. Spoon remaining ice cream on top, then remaining chocolate mixture; freeze. Sprinkle with nuts.

Rose Donahue (Mrs. Gerald)

Frozen Ice Cream Pie

Serves 6-8

¼ c. brown sugar
1 c. flour, sifted
½ c. chopped walnuts
½ c. melted butter
1 c. chocolate bits
1 c. evaporated milk
1 c. marshmallows
1 t. salt
½ gal. coffee ice cream
chopped walnuts

Combine first four ingredients; press onto bottom and sides of a greased 10″ deep dish pie pan. Bake at 350° for 20 minutes. Melt next four ingredients in top of double boiler; cool. Spread half of the ice cream over crust. Add half of the chocolate mixture; freeze. Add remaining ice cream and chocolate. Sprinkle with walnuts. Cover with foil, freeze. Refrigerate 10 minutes before serving.

Mary Demetriou (Mrs. Theodore)

Pumpkin Ice Cream Pie

Serves 6-8

1⅔ c. gingersnap
  crumbs
¼ c. butter, melted
¼ c. sugar
1 envelope unflavored
  gelatin
¼ c. cold water
½ c. canned pumpkin
¼ t. ginger
1½ t. cinnamon
1 t. vanilla
1 qt. vanilla ice cream,
  softened

Combine crumbs, butter and sugar; reserve ½ cup for topping. Press remaining crumbs into a 9″ pie plate; freeze. Soften gelatin in water; add to pumpkin. Stir in seasonings; cook over low heat until gelatin is dissolved. Cool. Mix with ice cream. Spoon into pie shell; sprinkle with reserved crumbs; freeze. Remove from freezer before serving to facilitate cutting.

Eleanor Pappky (Mrs. Herbert)

Creamy Lemon Pie

Serves 6-8

1½ c. lemon wafer
  crumbs
1 T. sugar
¼ c. butter, melted
1 6 oz. can lemonade
  concentrate, thawed
1 qt. vanilla ice cream,
  softened
lemon slices
mint sprigs

Combine crumbs, sugar and butter; press into bottom and sides of 9″ pie plate; bake at 300° for 12-15 minutes; cool; chill. Beat lemonade into ice cream; spoon into crust; freeze at least 4 hours. Garnish with lemon and mint.

Charlanne Lamberto (Mrs. Victor)

Sour Cream-Lemon Pie

Serves 6-8

1 c. sugar
3 T. cornstarch
¼ c. butter
1 T. lemon rind, grated
¼ c. lemon juice
3 egg yolks
1 c. milk
1 c. sour cream
1 9″ pie shell, baked
heavy cream, whipped
chopped walnuts

Combine sugar and cornstarch; add butter, lemon rind and juice. Beat in egg yolks; stir in milk; cook over medium heat, stirring constantly, until thickened; cool. Fold in sour cream. Spoon into pie shell; chill at least 2 hours. Garnish with cream and walnuts.

Isobel Mitchell (Mrs. James)

Hawaiian Bavarian Pie

Serves 8

2 c. oatmeal cookie
   crumbs
¼ c. butter, melted
1 envelope unflavored
   gelatin
¼ c. cold water
½ c. sugar
3 eggs, separated
¾ c. milk
¼ t. salt
1 c. heavy cream,
   whipped
1 c. coconut
1 c. crushed pineapple,
   drained
green food coloring
   (optional)

Combine crumbs and butter; press into bottom and sides of 10″ pie plate; bake at 350° for 5 minutes. Soften gelatin in water. In top of double boiler, combine ¼ c. sugar, beaten egg yolks, gelatin and milk; cook until thickened; chill, stirring occasionally while mixture continues to thicken. Beat egg whites with salt until foamy; gradually add remaining sugar; fold into gelatin mixture. Fold in cream, pineapple and ½ c. coconut. Pour into crust; sprinkle with remaining coconut, tinted with coloring. Serve chilled.

Joan Higgins

Mocha Chiffon Pie

Serves 6-8

1 c. coconut, lightly
   toasted
1 c. vanilla wafer
   crumbs
⅓ c. butter, softened
½ c. + 2 T. sugar
1¼ c. milk
3 eggs, separated
2 T. powdered instant
   coffee
⅛ t. salt
1 square unsweetened
   chocolate, melted
1 envelope unflavored
   gelatin
1 t. vanilla
½ c. heavy cream,
   whipped

Combine coconut crumbs, butter and 2 T. of the sugar. Press into bottom and sides of a 9″ pie plate, making a small rim; bake at 350° for 10 minutes until golden brown. In a 2 qt. saucepan combine milk, egg yolks, coffee, salt and ¼ cup sugar; beat well with wisk; add chocolate; sprinkle gelatin over mixture; cook over low heat, stirring constantly, until thickened and mixture coats spoon (do not boil). Add vanilla; refrigerate 40 minutes until cold but not set. Gradually sprinkle remaining sugar into softly beaten egg whites until dissolved. Fold mixtures together gently. Spoon into crust; chill 1 hour or until set. Decorate with whipped cream.

Janet Crandlemire (Mrs. Roger)

Macadamia Nut Rum Pie

Serves 6-8

3 eggs
½ c. sugar
1 c. light corn syrup
¼ c. butter, melted
2 T. Jamaican rum
1 t. vanilla
1 c. finely chopped
  macadamia nuts
⅔ c. chopped dates
1 9″ pie shell, unbaked
vanilla ice cream

Beat first 6 ingredients together; stir in nuts and dates. Turn into pie shell; bake at 375° for 40 minutes until filling is set; cool on rack. Top with ice cream. (Very rich)

Jane Potter (Mrs. Howard)

Mystery Pecan Pie

Serves 6-8

1 8 oz. pkg. cream
  cheese
⅓ c. + ¼ c. sugar
¼ t. salt
2 t. vanilla
4 eggs
1 9″ or 10″ pie shell,
  unbaked
1¼ c. chopped pecans
1 c. light corn syrup

Combine cream cheese, ⅓ cup sugar, salt, 1 t. of the vanilla and 1 egg; pour into pie shell. Sprinkle with pecans. Combine remaining eggs, sugar, vanilla and syrup; pour over pecans. Bake at 375° for 35-40 minutes until center is firm.

Marge Pachuta (Mrs. Roger)

Peach Custard Pie

Serves 6-8

1½ c. + 2 T. instant
  presifted flour
½ t. salt
½ c. butter, softened
2 T. + ⅓ c. sour cream
6 large peaches, pared,
  sliced
3 egg yolks
1 c. sugar

Mix 1¼ cups flour, salt, butter and 2 T. sour cream; pat into bottom and sides of 9″ pie plate; bake at 425° for 10 minutes. Put peaches in pie shell. Mix egg yolks, sugar, remaining flour and sour cream; spoon on top of peaches; cover with foil. Bake at 350° for 35-45 minutes; remove foil, bake an additional 10 minutes until custard is set.

Anne Urban (Mrs. Robert)

Peanut Butter Pie

Serves 6-8

⅔ c. brown sugar,
  packed
½ t. salt
½ t. nutmeg
1 t. cinnamon
⅛ t. ground cloves
¼ t. ginger
3 eggs, separated
½ c. light cream
1½ c. canned pumpkin
½ c. peanut butter
1 envelope unflavored
  gelatin
½ c. cold water
1 9″ pie shell, baked
heavy cream, whipped

In double boiler combine sugar, salt, spices, beaten egg yolks, cream, pumpkin and peanut butter; cook until hot, stirring constantly. Soak gelatin in water for 5 minutes; add to pumpkin mixture; chill. When mixture begins to thicken, fold in stiffly beaten egg whites. Pour into pie shell; chill at least 4 hours. Garnish with cream.

Libby Porter (Mrs. Robert)

Peanut Streusel Pie

Serves 6-8

⅓ c. peanut butter
¾ c. confectioners sugar
1 9″ pie shell, baked
⅓ c. flour
1 c. sugar, divided
⅛ t. salt
2 c. milk, scalded
3 eggs, separated
2 T. butter
½ t. vanilla
¼ t. cream of tartar
1 T. cornstarch

Blend peanut butter and confectioners sugar until mealy; sprinkle ⅔ into pie shell. Combine flour, ¼ c. sugar and salt in double boiler; stir in milk; cook until thickened. Stir in egg yolks gradually; cook a few minutes; add butter and vanilla; cool slightly; pour into pie shell. Beat egg whites until foamy; add cream of tartar, cornstarch and remaining sugar gradually, beating well between additions until stiff. Spread meringue on top of pie; sprinkle with remaining peanut butter and sugar mixture. Bake at 350° for 15 minutes; cool. Serve chilled.

Jane Nocito (Mrs. Mark)
Sara Sellers (Mrs. Dean)

Strawberry Cheese Pie

Serves 6-8

1 9" pie shell, baked
1 3 oz. pkg. cream
    cheese, softened
whole fresh strawberries
2 c. strawberries,
    mashed
1 c. sugar
3½ T. cornstarch
½ pt. heavy cream,
    whipped

Line pie shell with cream cheese; place whole berries in bottom. Combine mashed berries, sugar and cornstarch; bring to boil; cook until thickened and clear. Pour over fresh berries; chill. Garnish with cream.

Thelma Gee (Mrs. Harold)

Surprise Pie

Serves 6-8

3 egg whites, stiffly
    beaten
1 c. sugar
1 t. baking powder
1 t. vanilla
20 Ritz crackers,
    crushed
½ c. walnuts, chopped
heavy cream, whipped

Combine stiffly beaten egg whites, sugar, baking powder and vanilla; stir in crackers and walnuts. Spread in an ungreased 9" pie plate; bake at 350° for 30 minutes. Garnish with cream.

Pat Sayles (Mrs. Thomas)

Freda's Peach Kuchen

Serves 6-8

¾ c. butter
¼ c. sugar
2 c. flour
¼ t. baking powder
½ t. salt
2 eggs, beaten, divided
milk
peaches, sliced
¼ c. heavy cream
2-3 T. sugar or to taste

Blend butter and sugar; add flour, baking powder and salt with a pastry blender. Add one of the eggs and enough milk to form a pliable dough. Dough should be somewhat crumbly. Roll on lightly floured surface; place in a greased 9" pie plate. Top with peaches; spread with combined cream, remaining egg and sugar. Bake at 350° for 30 minutes.

Suzanne Koerner (Mrs. Leonard)

Blueberry Tart

1 c. flour
2 T. confectioners sugar
½ c. butter
2 c. blueberries
1 10 oz. jar currant jelly
2 T. walnuts, toasted, chopped finely
1 c. sour cream

Sift flour and sugar together; cut in butter with pastry blender until mixture resembles cornmeal; chill 20 minutes; turn into a greased 9" tart or pie pan; press crust firmly on bottom and sides. Bake at 425° for 10-12 minutes until golden brown; cool on rack. Spread berries on crust. Melt jelly over low heat; cool; spoon over berries; chill until jelly is well set. Sprinkle walnuts around edges; drop sour cream in blobs over berries, not covering nuts. Serve chilled.

Dottie Stevens (Mrs. Roger)

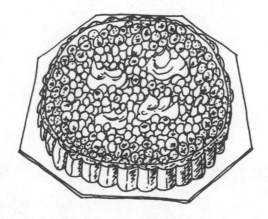

Rhubarb Tart

2 c. + 5 T. flour
½ t. salt
1½ t. baking powder
7 T. + 1½ c. sugar
¼ c. milk
¾ c. butter
4 c. diced rhubarb
3 eggs, separated

Combine 2 cups of the flour, salt, baking powder, 1 tablespoon of the sugar, milk and butter with pastry blender. Press into bottom and sides of an 11½" pan, using fingers. Combine rhubarb, remaining flour, 1½ cups of the sugar and beaten egg yolks; pour over crust. Bake at 425° for 30 minutes; cool. Combine stiffly beaten egg whites and remaining sugar; spread over rhubarb. Bake at 425° until top is lightly browned.

Mary Kay Reber (Mrs. George)

Fruit Strudel

Serves 6-8

1 c. butter, softened
1 c. vanilla ice cream,
    softened
2 c. flour
1 8 oz. jar apricot jam
golden raisins
chopped pecans

Combine butter, ice cream and flour; refrigerate overnight. Roll out dough very thinly. Spread with jam; sprinkle with raisins and pecans. Roll. Put on greased cookie sheet. Cut halfway through at 1 inch intervals. Bake at 350° for 30 minutes.

Ann Brink (Mrs. Raymond)
Joanne Keith (Mrs. James)

Mincemeat Strudel

Serves 6

1 medium apple, pared,
    finely chopped
1 9 oz. pkg. condensed
    mincemeat
1 T. sugar
1 c. water
⅓ c. butter, melted,
    cooled
4 phyllo sheets

Combine apple, mincemeat, sugar and water; stir over medium heat for 5 minutes; cool. Place 1 phyllo sheet on a tea towel; brush lightly with butter. Layer remaining phyllo sheets on top of first, brushing each with butter. Place mincemeat mixture along one short edge of pastry. Using the towel to help you, roll up pastry like a jelly roll tucking sides under so that filling will remain encased. Place seam side down on buttered cookie sheet. Brush with butter. Make three evenly spaced ½" long cuts on top of strudel. Bake at 350° for 30-35 minutes or until golden brown. Serve warm.

Claire Hadden (Mrs. William)

Cream Cheese Pastries

½ lb. butter, softened
8 oz. cream cheese, softened
¼ t. salt
2 c. flour, sifted

Filling:
1 c. chopped walnuts
½ c. sugar
1 t. cinnamon
½ t. lemon rind
¼ c. milk, heated to boiling
confectioners sugar

Optional Fillings:
¾ c. raspberry or apricot preserves
drained crushed pineapple sweetened with sugar
prune butter
prune preserves mixed with grated orange or lemon rind

Mix butter and cream cheese until creamy; mix in salt and flour. Divide into 3 equal portions; wrap in waxed paper; refrigerate at least 2 hours or overnight. Roll out one portion at a time on lightly floured surface; cut into 2½" squares. Combine walnuts, sugar, cinnamon and lemon rind; add milk. Place ¼ t. of filling into center of each square; press opposite corners together moistening lightly with water to seal, or roll each portion into ⅛" thick circles; cut each into wedges. Place filling in center and starting at long edge, roll to form a crescent. Bake on an ungreased cookie sheet at 350° for 15 minutes until lightly browned. Cool on rack; sprinkle with confectioners sugar if desired.

Kay Dowd (Mrs. Russell)
Lynn Ferentchak (Mrs. Rudy)
Jean Richardson (Mrs. A.J.)
Edna Vogel (Mrs. Nathan)

Sour Cream Pastries

1 c. butter
2 c. flour, sifted
1 egg yolks, beaten
½ c. sour cream
½ c. apricot preserves
½ c. coconut
¼ c. pecans, finely chopped

Cut butter into flour until mixture resembles fine crumbs. Combine egg yolk and sour cream; blend into flour mixture. Chill several hours or overnight. Divide dough into 4 equal portions; keep refrigerated until ready to use. Roll each to a 10" circle on lightly floured surface. Spread each with 2 T. preserves, 2 T. coconut and 1 T. pecans. Cut each circle into 12 wedges with fluted pastry wheel. From wide end, roll each into a crescent. Sprinkle with sugar. Bake on an ungreased cookie sheet at 350° for 20 minutes until lightly browned. Cool on rack. May be frozen.

Joan Holmes (Mrs. Richard)

Desserts

Broiler Baked Alaska

Serves 4

3 **egg whites**
6 **T. sugar**
salt
1 **pt. peach ice cream**
4 **individual sponge cake dessert cups**
4 **t. peach brandy**

Beat egg whites until soft peaks form; add sugar and salt, beating until stiff peaks form. Place a scoop of ice cream in each sponge cake cup, making a hollow in center of ice cream; pour 1 teaspoon brandy into each. Spread ¼ of the meringue over each, spreading to edge of cake; freeze. Broil until lightly browned.

Berkeley Hayes (Mrs. William)

Angel Meringue Dessert

Serves 6-8

4 **egg whites**
⅛ **t. salt**
¼ **t. cream of tartar**
1½ **c. sugar, divided**
1 **10 oz. pkg. frozen sliced strawberries, drained (reserve juice)**
2 **T. cornstarch**
¼ **c. cold water**
½ **pt. heavy cream, whipped**

Beat egg whites and salt until frothy; beat in cream of tartar until soft peaks form; gradually beat in 1 cup of the sugar. Spread in bottom of a well-greased and floured 9" pie plate. Bake at 300° for 1 hour; cool. Combine reserved juice from berries with remaining sugar; stir in cornstarch mixed with water. Cook until thickened; add berries; cool. Spread some of the whipped cream on meringue; spoon on strawberry mixture. Top with remaining whipped cream; chill.

Ann Harrison (Mrs. Thomas)

Alternate topping:
4 **egg yolks, beaten**
3 **T. lemon juice**
½ **c. sugar**
1 **t. grated lemon rind**
½ **pt. heavy cream, whipped**

Prepare meringue as above. Combine all ingredients except whipped cream. Cook until thickened; cool. Fold in whipped cream; spread on meringue; chill.

Alice Ashurst

Forgotten Dessert

Serves 10

5 egg whites
¼ t. salt
½ t. cream of tartar
1½ c. sugar
1 t. vanilla
½ pt. cream
1 t. powdered sugar

Beat egg whites until foamy. Add cream of tartar; beat until stiff. Add sugar a little at a time, then vanilla; beat 15 minutes. Spread mixture in greased 11x7" glass dish. Put in 450° oven; turn off heat; go to bed. Remove from oven next morning; spread with cream whipped with powdered sugar. Refrigerate. To serve, cut in squares topped with fresh fruit.

Mabel Ehlert (Mrs. William)

Bavarian Grand Marnier

Serves 6-8

2 envelopes unflavored
   gelatin
1¾ c. water, divided
¼ c. sugar
1 6 oz. can frozen
   orange juice, thawed
salt
¼-½ c. Grand Marnier
1 c. heavy cream,
   whipped
orange sections

Sprinkle gelatin over 1 cup of the water; add sugar, heat until gelatin is dissolved. Add remaining water, orange juice, salt and Grand Marnier. Chill until slightly thickened. Fold in cream. Pour into a 6 cup mold or 6-8 individual serving dishes; chill until firm. Garnish with orange sections.

Carolyn Milne (Mrs. Jack)

Cheesecake Pie

Serves 6

2 8 oz. pkgs. cream
   cheese, softened
3 eggs
⅔ c. + 3 T. sugar
⅛ t. almond extract
2 c. sour cream
1 t. vanilla
shaved Brazil nuts or
   slivered almonds

Beat cream cheese until creamy; add eggs one at a time, beating after each addition. Beat in ⅔ cup of the sugar and almond extract for 5 minutes until smooth, thickened and lemon-colored. Bake in a greased 9" pie plate at 325° for 50 minutes; cool for 20 minutes. Beat sour cream with remaining sugar and vanilla; spoon over cheese cake. Bake at 325° for 15 minutes; cool to room temperature; sprinkle with nuts.

Anne Keyko (Mrs. George)

No-bake Cherry Cheesecake

Serves 12-14

2 c. graham cracker
  crumbs
3 T. sugar
¼ lb. butter, melted
2 8 oz. pkgs. cream
  cheese, softened
2 c. confectioners sugar
2 envelopes whipped
  topping mix
1 c. milk
1 t. vanilla
2 21 oz. cans cherry pie
  filling

Combine crumbs, sugar and butter; press into a 13x9" glass pan. Blend cream cheese and confectioners sugar together. Prepare whipped topping mix with milk and vanilla according to package directions. Fold into cream cheese mixture; spread on crust. Top with cherry pie filling; chill.

Carol Beasley (Mrs. David)

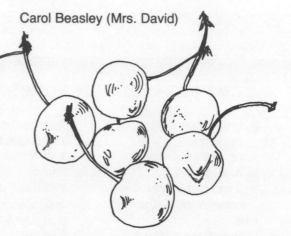

Hazelnut Torte

Serves 8

8 T. sugar
8 eggs, separated
10 T. ground hazelnuts
  or walnuts, divided
3 T. bread crumbs
salt

Filling:
½ lb. unsalted butter,
  softened
6 T. confectioners sugar
1½-2 oz. rum
2 egg yolks
whole hazelnuts or
  walnuts

Gradually beat sugar into egg yolks until thick and lemon-colored. Gently stir in 8 tablespoons of the nuts, one tablespoon at a time. Gently stir in crumbs, one tablespoon at a time. Stiffly beat egg whites with salt; fold into nut mixture, one fourth at a time. Bake in 2 greased and floured 8 or 9" cake pans at 350° for 30-40 minutes. Cool on wire racks; split each cake in half.

Filling: Cream butter and confectioners sugar together; gradually add rum, egg yolks and remaining nuts; spread between all 4 cake layers and on top and sides. Decorate with whole nuts; chill, covered.

Lilian Goodwin (Mrs. Elmer)

Frozen Chocolate Dessert

Serves 8

6 T. butter, melted
18 Oreos, crushed
1 qt. vanilla ice cream, softened
1 T. instant powdered coffee
1 5½ oz. can evaporated milk
1½ oz. bitter chocolate
½ c. sugar
⅓ c. chopped nuts

Pour butter over cookies in an 11x8" pan. Combine ice cream and coffee; spread over cookies; freeze. Combine milk, chocolate and sugar; cook until slightly thickened. Cool; spread over ice cream. Sprinkle with nuts; refreeze.

Marge Pachuta (Mrs. Roger)

Chocolate Meringue Torte

Serves 8-10

5 egg whites, room temperature
¼ t. cream of tartar
¾ c. sugar
1 t. vanilla, divided
1 c. semi-sweet chocolate mini-chips
¼ c. finely chopped nuts
18 marshmallows
⅓ c. water
⅛ t. salt
3 egg yolks, beaten
1 6 oz. pkg. semi-sweet chocolate chips
½ c. heavy cream, whipped

Beat egg whites until frothy; add cream of tartar; beat until soft peaks form. Gradually add sugar, beating until stiff. Beat in ½ teaspoon of the vanilla; fold in chocolate and nuts. Butter 4 7" circles of foil or brown paper placed on cookie sheet. Spread each circle with meringue mixture; bake at 200° for 1 hour. Cool in oven for 2 hours; peel off foil. Combine marshmallows, water and salt; cook over low heat until melted and smooth, stirring constantly; add small amount to egg yolks. Add egg yolks to marshmallow mixture; cook 1 minute, stirring constantly. Add chocolate chips, stirring until melted and smooth. Cool for 5 minutes. Fold in cream and remaining vanilla; chill until thick enough to spread. Stack meringues with chocolate mixture between each; chill. Garnish with additional whipped cream and chopped nuts.

Nancy Brink (Mrs. Ronald)

Chocolate-Coconut Dessert

Serves 16

1 6 oz. pkg. semi-sweet
  chocolate bits
1 13 oz. can evaporated
  milk
1 10½ oz. pkg.
  miniature
  marshmallows
1⅓ c. coconut
6 T. butter
2 c. dry rice cereal,
  crushed
1 c. chopped walnuts
½ gal. vanilla ice cream,
  softened

Melt chocolate in milk; boil gently for four minutes until thickened, stirring constantly. Stir in marshmallows; head until melted; chill. Lightly brown coconut in butter; stir in cereal and walnuts; spread 3 cups of cereal mixture in bottom of a 13x9″ pan. Spread with half of the ice cream, then half of the chocolate mixture. Repeat layers; top with cereal mixture. Cover; freeze. Let stand at room temperature for 10 minutes to soften before serving.

June McCann (Mrs. John)

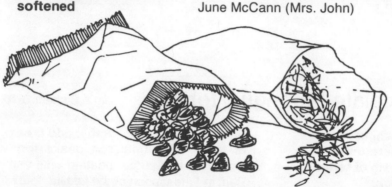

Nubian Chocolate Roll

Serves 4-6

3 eggs, separated
5 T. + ¼ c. sugar
5 T. cocoa, divided
1½ t. vanilla, divided
½ t. almond extract
½ t. cinnamon
1 c. heavy cream
shaved chocolate
chopped nuts

Beat egg yolks; add 5 tablespoons sugar, 3 tablespoons cocoa, 1 teaspoon vanilla, almond extract and cinnamon; beat until creamy. Fold in beaten egg whites; pour into a greased 8″ square pan, lined with waxed paper. Bake at 350° for 25 minutes. Cool in pan for 5 minutes; turn out, cool an additional 5 minutes before removing waxed paper; cool completely. Whip cream with remaining sugar, cocoa and vanilla. Spread some on cake; roll cake, jelly roll fashion. Spread remaining filling on top and sides. Sprinkle with chocolate and nuts.

Mary Kay Reber (Mrs. George)

Chocolate Mousse Tartlets

Yield: 36

1 c. vanilla wafer
   crumbs (reserve 5-6 t.
   for topping)
1 c. butter, softened
2 c. sifted
   confectioners sugar
4 oz. unsweetened
   chocolate, melted,
   cooled
4 eggs, beaten
2 t. vanilla
1-2 T. rum or brandy

Place a layer of crumbs into bottoms of 36 miniature paper cup cake liners. Beat butter and sugar together until fluffy; beat in chocolate, eggs, vanilla and rum. Spoon into cup cake liners; top with reserved crumbs; freeze. Serve frozen.

Grace Heerwagen (Mrs. Elwood)

Cranberry Sour Cream Tarts

Serves 6

1 egg, beaten
2 T. butter, melted
milk
2 c. biscuit mix
1 pt. sour cream
1 c. sugar
1 t. cinnamon
½ t. nutmeg
2 c. coarsely chopped
   cranberries

Combine egg and butter; add enough milk to measure ¾ cup; stir into biscuit mix. Spread over bottom of an 8″ pan; bake at 450° for 10 minutes. Combine sour cream, sugar, cinnamon and nutmeg; fold in cranberries; spread over dough. Bake at 375° for 15-20 minutes until center is set. Let stand for 10 minutes before cutting. Serve warm or cold.

Eleanor B. Mason

Liqueur-flavored Ice Cream

Serves 10-12

4 oz. brandy or 5 oz.
   almond liqueur
1-4 oz. crème de cacoa
½ gal. vanilla ice cream,
   softened

Blend liqueurs and ice cream; refreeze.

Jean Lum (Mrs. Frederick H., III)
Betty Gorman (Mrs. Paul)

Apricot Mousse

2 pkgs. lady fingers,
  split
1 1 lb. can apricots,
  pitted, drained
  (reserve liquid)
water
2 3 oz. pkgs. lemon
  gelatin
2 T. apricot brandy or
  Cointreau
2 c. heavy cream,
  whipped
apricot halves
heavy cream, whipped

Line bottom and sides of a 10″ spring form pan with lady fingers. Combine reserved apricot liquid with enough water to measure 3½ cups. Heat to boiling; add gelatin, stirring to dissolve. Purée apricots in blender; add to gelatin mixture; add brandy. Chill until slightly thickened. Beat slightly; fold in cream. Pour over lady fingers. Chill for 3 hours until set. Garnish with apricot halves and additional whipped cream.

Betty Ziegler (Mrs. John)

Frozen Maple Mousse

2 egg yolks
⅛ t. salt
1¼ c. maple syrup
2 c. heavy cream,
  whipped
heavy cream

Beat egg yolks with salt until lemon-colored. Heat syrup until slightly bubbling around edges of pan; beat into eggs. Cook in top of double boiler over simmering water until mixture coats spoon, stirring constantly. Set top of double boiler in ice water; beat until thick, fluffy and chilled; fold in cream. Pour into 2 ice cube trays; freeze until firmed 1″ from edges. Transfer to bowl; beat with whisk until smooth. Turn into a 6 cup mold; freeze covered, at least 8 hours until firm. Garnish with additional whipped cream.

Polly Ward (Mrs. Robertson)

Frozen Orange Souffle

Serves 8

6 egg yolks
¾ c. sugar
2¾ c. heavy cream,
    whipped, divided
3-4 oz. orange-flavored
    liqueur
8 oranges
powdered cocoa

Beat egg yolks and sugar together until stiff; fold in 2 cups of the whipped cream; add liqueur. Cut the tops off the oranges; scoop out pulp and membranes. Fill orange shells with cream mixture; freeze at least 2 hours. Top with reserved whipped cream; sprinkle with cocoa. (Muffin tins lined with paper liners or souffle cups may be substituted for orange shells.)

Donna Walcott (Mrs. John)

Cold Sherry Souffle

Serves 12

2 envelopes unflavored
    gelatin
1½ c. sweet sherry
6 eggs, separated
¾ c. sugar, divided
1 T. lemon juice
½ c. cold water
1 c. heavy cream
lady fingers

Soften gelatin in cold water for 5 minutes. Place over boiling water; stir until dissolved. Remove from heat; add sherry. Cool. Chill for 30 minutes until mixture begins to thicken. Beat egg whites until foamy. Add ½ cup sugar gradually, beating constantly. Add lemon juice; beat until mixture is stiff, but not dry. Beat egg yolks until frothy, add remaining sugar gradually; beat until yolks are thick and lemon colored. Add slightly thickened gelatin slowly to egg yolks; continue beating until thick and light. Fold beaten egg whites into gelatin mixture. Whip cream; fold in. Pour into a collared 7″ souffle dish, lined with lady fingers. Chill for 3 hours until firm. Remove paper collar before serving. Serve with additional whipped cream if desired.

Virginia L. Campbell

Lemon Fromage

Serves 8

3 eggs, separated
½ c. + 3 T. sugar
1 envelope unflavored gelatin
¼ c. cold water
¼ c. lemon juice
2 t. lemon peel
1 c. heavy cream, whipped
2 pkgs. lady fingers, split
1 t. confectioners sugar
1 lemon, thinly sliced

Beat egg yolks with ½ cup of the sugar until lemon colored. In top of double boiler, melt gelatin in water until completely dissolved. Combine with egg yolks; add lemon juice and peel; fold in cream. Beat egg whites until stiff, gradually adding remaining sugar. Fold into cream mixture. Line bottom and sides of an 11x8" pan with lady fingers; pour in fromage mixture. Sprinkle with confectioners sugar; garnish with lemon slices; chill.

Lucy Meyer (Mrs. Wallace)

Lemon Sponge Pudding

Serves 6

2 T. butter, softened
1 c. sugar
3 eggs, separated
¼ c. flour
⅛ t. salt
1 T. grated lemon rind
⅓ c. lemon juice
1½ c. milk
heavy cream, whipped

Cream butter and sugar together; stir in beaten egg yolks, flour, salt, rind and juice. Fold in stiffly beaten egg whites; pour into a greased 1½ quart baking dish. Set in shallow pan of hot water; bake at 350° for 45-60 minutes until set. Serve warm or cold, garnished with cream.

Helen Campbell (Mrs. D.J.)
Claire Rushin (Mrs. Robert)

Almond Apple Crisp

Serves 6

2 lbs. tart cooking apples
1⅓ c. sugar
1 c. flour
¼ t. cinnamon
⅔ c. chopped almonds
½ c. butter, melted
1 t. vanilla
1 c. heavy cream, whipped

Peel and core apples; cut into ½ inch slices. Spread in buttered shallow 2 quart baking dish. Combine sugar, flour and cinnamon; stir in almonds. Mix butter and vanilla; stir into almond mixture until crumbly. Sprinkle evenly over apples. Bake at 400° for 30-40 minutes until topping is browned and apples are tender. Partially cool on rack. Top each serving with whipped cream.

Jane Potter (Mrs. Howard)

"Banana Split"

½ lb. butter, softened, divided
2 c. graham cracker crumbs
¼ c. sugar
2 c. confectioners sugar
2 eggs
1 t. vanilla
1 16 oz. can crushed pineapple, well drained
6 bananas, sliced
3 10 oz. pkgs. frozen sliced strawberries, well drained (reserve juice)
heavy cream, whipped
chopped nuts

Combine ¼ pound of the butter, crumbs and sugar; press into bottom of a 13x9" pan. Bake at 375° for 8 minutes. With electric mixer or blender, beat confectioners sugar, eggs, vanilla and remaining butter for 20 minutes until creamy. Spread on crust. Cover with pineapple; lay banana slices on top. Thicken reserved strawberry juice with cornstarch and water; add strawberries. Spoon over bananas. Top with cream and nuts. (May be made ahead of time and topped with whipped cream when ready to serve.)

Grace Heerwagen (Mrs. Elwood)

Peaches and Cream Cheese Cobbler

Serves 6

¾ c. flour
1 t. baking powder
½ t. salt
1 pkg. vanilla pudding
3 T. butter
1 egg
½ c. milk
1 15 oz. can sliced peaches

Filling:
1 8 oz. pkg. cream cheese
1 c. sugar
3 T. peach juice

Topping:
1 T. sugar
½ t. cinnamon

Combine first six ingredients. Beat 2 minutes at medium speed. Pour into greased 9" pie dish. Add sliced peaches.

Filling: Combine all ingredients and beat at medium speed for 2-3 minutes. Spoon on top of peaches leaving 1 inch around edge.

Topping: Combine sugar and cinnamon; sprinkle over top. Bake at 350° for 30-40 minutes. Must be cooled at least 2-3 hours before serving.

Susan Nelson

Peach Pudding

Serves 6-8

1⅓ c. sugar, divided
¼ c. butter, softened
1 t. salt, divided
1 t. baking powder
1 c. flour
½ c. milk
2 c. pared, sliced
   peaches or apples
1 T. cornstarch
1 c. boiling water

Combine ⅔ cup sugar, butter, baking powder and ½ teaspoon salt. Beat in flour and milk alternately with electric mixer. Place fruit in a greased 2 quart or 10x6″ baking dish; spread with batter, not covering fruit completely. Combine remaining sugar and salt with cornstarch, sprinkle over batter; pour water over all. Bake at 350° for 30-35 minutes. Serve warm with vanilla ice cream, if desired.

Mary Ellen Tully (Mrs. Thomas)

Grapefruit Granité

Serves 8

2 c. sugar
peeled rind of 1 orange
peeled rind of ½ lemon
2 c. water
2½ c. grapefruit juice
⅔ c. orange juice
1 T. lemon juice
1 T. rum or ¼ c. vodka
maraschino cherries

Heat sugar, rinds and water until sugar is dissolved; simmer 4 minutes; strain; cool. Add juices and rum; add additional sugar to sweeten, if desired. Chill. Turn into 2 ice cube trays; freeze until firm. Stir and spoon into chilled sherbert glasses; top each with a cherry. (If vodka is used, 1 tablespoon of vodka over each portion makes it interesting!)

Jean Tardiff (Mrs. Charles)

Gingered Blueberry Compote

Serves 6

1 c. orange juice
1 T. lemon juice
¼ c. confectioners sugar
2 T. minced preserved
   ginger
1 pt. blueberries
mint leaves

Combine orange and lemon juices, sugar and ginger; pour over berries; chill for 1-2 hours. Garnish with mint leaves.

Margaret Gloeckner

Melon in Champagne

Serves 4-6

1 large ripe cantaloupe
dry champagne

Cut off top end of cantaloupe, about 1½". Scoop out flesh with a melon baller. Place back into the shell. Pour enough champagne into the cavity to cover the melon. Replace top; chill.

Eileen Shea

Pineapple Romanoff

Serves 8

1 pineapple, halved
   lengthwise
sugar
3 T. white rum
3 T. Cointreau
3 T. kirsch
½ pt. heavy cream,
   whipped

Remove pulp from pineapple; cut into cubes. Sweeten with sugar; add rum and Cointreau. Marinate in refrigerator; spoon into pineapple shells; top with combined kirsch and cream.

Greta Laughlin (Mrs. Richard)

Raspberry Ginger

Serves 8

1 c. sifted brown sugar
½ t. ginger
1½ pts. heavy cream,
   whipped
3 10 oz. pkgs. frozen
   raspberries, thawed,
   drained

Combine sugar and ginger; fold into cream; gently fold in berries; chill at least 1 hour. Before serving, gently restir.

Pat Brown (Mrs. Phillip)

Strawberries Romanoff

Serves 8

2 c. strawberries
¼ c. sugar
1 c. heavy cream, stiffly
   beaten
½ pt. vanilla ice cream,
   beaten until fluffy
¼ c. Cointreau

Sprinkle berries with sugar; chill at least 2 hours. Fold cream into ice cream, gently stir in Cointreau. Spoon over berries, stirring gently.

Jean Byrne (Mrs. Brendan T.)

Special Diets

Lemon Chicken

Serves 4

3 lbs. chicken parts
½ c. flour
¼ t. pepper
2 t. paprika
½ c. sweet butter, melted
½ t. pepper
¼ c. vegetable oil
½ c. lemon juice
2 t. grated lemon rind

Dredge chicken parts with combined flour, pepper and paprika. Arrange, skin side down, in a single layer in large greased baking dish. Combine remaining ingredients; spoon over chicken. Bake, uncovered, at 400° for 30 minutes. Turn chicken pieces; bake 20 minutes longer, basting occasionally. (Low Cholesterol)

Greta Laughlin (Mrs. Richard)

Veal Scallops with Lemon

Serves 4-6

2 lbs. veal scallops,
   pounded thin,
   seasoned with pepper
   and flour
6 T. unsalted margarine
¼ c. white wine
juice of one lemon
¼ c. Egg Beaters
parsley, lemon slices

Brown veal in margarine, a few pieces at a time. Return all pieces to pan; add wine and lemon juice. Cover; simmer for 6-7 minutes until veal is tender. Remove meat to heated platter. Scrape drippings from bottom of pan. Beat in Egg Beaters to thicken over low heat, and spoon over veal. Sprinkle with chopped parsley; garnish with lemon slices. (Low Cholesterol-Low Sodium)

Alice Stonaker (Mrs. Robert)

Meatless Chili

Serves 6-8

2 c. GranBurger or other
   vegetable burger*
1 bouillon cube
½ c. hot water
6 c. canned kidney
   beans
3½ c. tomatoes
2 onions, sliced
2 t. Kitchen Bouquet
2 T. sugar
2 t. chili powder
¼ t. pepper
¼ t. monosodium
   glutamate

Mix vegetable burger with bouillon cube dissolved in hot water; let stand 15 minutes. Combine remaining ingredients in large saucepan or dutch oven. Add vegetable burger mixture. Cook 1-2 hours over low heat. Freezes well. (Low Cholesterol)

Helen Fromel (Mrs. Robert)

*available in health food stores

Baked Lasagna

Serves 6-8

2 lbs. ground round
   steak (buy round
   steaks and ask
   butcher to trim fat and
   grind)
1 garlic clove, crushed
2 T. chopped parsley
2 T. dried basil
2 c. tomatoes
2 6 oz. cans tomato
   paste
8 lasagna noodles
   (Prince Lasagna has
   no salt and no
   cholesterol)
2 12 oz. cartons dry
   curd cottage cheese
   with no salt added
½ c. Egg Beaters
½ t. pepper
2 T. parsley
½ c. Parmesan cheese
1 lb. part-skim
   mozzarella cheese,
   grated

Brown meat; add next 5 ingredients. Simmer, uncovered, until thick for 45-60 minutes, stirring occasionally. Cook noodles until tender; drain; rinse. Combine cottage cheese with next 4 ingredients. Place 4 noodles in a 13x9" baking dish; spread with half the cheese mixture; add half mozzarella and half meat mixture. Repeat layers. Bako at 375° for 30-40 minutes. Let casserole sit for 15 minutes, covered with foil. (Low Cholesterol-Low Sodium)

Alice Stonaker (Mrs. Robert)

Johnny Marzetti

½ c. diced green pepper
1 c. diced onion
1 c. diced celery
1 15 oz. can tomato
  sauce
1 16 oz. can tomatoes
1 c. water
½ t. garlic powder
1 T. sugar
1 4 oz. can sliced
  mushrooms, drained
1½ c. vegetable burger*
8 oz. medium noodles,
  cooked
8 oz. Cheddar cheese,
  grated

Coat a dutch oven with cooking oil. Add pepper, onion and celery. Cover; cook 10 minutes until vegetables are tender. Add everything except noodles and cheese. Cover; simmer for 20 minutes. Combine noodles with sauce. Place in 3 quart casserole. Top with grated cheese. Bake, uncovered at 350° for 20 minutes. (Low Cholesterol)

Helen Fromel (Mrs. Robert)

*available in health food stores

Meatless Spaghetti Sauce

1½ c. GranBurger or
  other vegetable
  burger*
2 c. tomatoes
1 large onion, chopped
1 garlic clove, chopped
1 4 oz. can mushrooms
1 8 oz. can tomato
  sauce
1 sprig parsley,
  chopped
½ t. monosodium
  glutamate
⅛ t. pepper
1 can bouillon or 1
  bouillon cube
  dissolved in 1½ c. hot
  water
2 t. Kitchen Bouquet
½ t. chili powder

Combine ingredients in deep skillet or dutch oven. Cook over low heat for 45 minutes. Freezes well. (Low Cholesterol)

Helen Fromel (Mrs. Robert)

*available at health food stores

Pesto

2 c. coarsely chopped
    fresh basil leaves or 2
    c. coarsely chopped
    Italian parsley plus 2
    T. dried basil leaves
½ t. freshly ground black
    pepper
1-2 t. chopped peeled
    garlic
3 T. chopped pine nuts
    or walnuts
1 c. olive oil
½ c. Parmesan cheese
cooked spaghetti or
    linguini

Combine first five ingredients in blender at high speed until smooth. Turn off occasionally to scrape sides with rubber scraper. Heat sauce. Remove from heat; stir in cheese. Pour on spaghetti and toss. (Low Cholesterol-Low Sodium)

Joyce Margie (Mrs. Robert)

Low Fat Eggplant

2 medium eggplants,
    peeled, sliced ¼" thick
¼ c. water
1 c. fat-free cottage
    cheese
1 egg
4 oz. part skim
    mozzarella cheese,
    diced or shredded
2 T. Parmesan or
    Romano cheese
1 8 oz. can tomato
    sauce
salt, pepper
Italian Seasoning

Blanch and drain eggplant. Mix cottage cheese and egg together. Spray baking dish with cooking spray. Layer half the eggplant and tomato sauce; sprinkle with seasonings. Add half of cheese mixture and mozzarella. Repeat layers. Top with cheese. Bake at 350° for 35 minutes until bubbly. (Four 220 calorie servings or five 176 calorie servings — Low Fat)

Pat Habig (Mrs. Franklin)

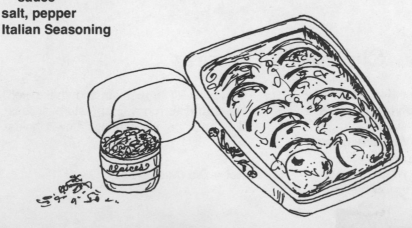

Spinach Frittata

1 t. chopped scallion
2 T. water
1 c. chopped spinach
2 eggs, beaten
1 t. dill
salt and pepper
1½ T. Parmesan cheese

Simmer scallion in water for a few minutes in small skillet. Spread spinach evenly over scallion; heat. Pour eggs over spinach. Cook slowly until egg is almost set. Add seasonings and cheese; place under broiler until puffed. (180 Calories — Low Fat)

Jo Waag (Mrs. William)

Low Fat Dressing

¼ c. buttermilk
2 T. lemon juice
2 T. ketchup
1 t. onion juice

Combine all ingredients.
(It's better than you think!)

Deborah-Ann Sappah

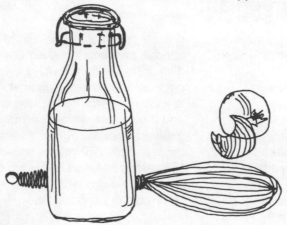

Low Cholesterol Dressing

½ c. salad oil,
   polyunsaturated
2 T. sugar
1 t. Worcestershire
   sauce
¼ c. white vinegar
½ T. onion flakes

Combine all ingredients and shake well. Let stand at room temperature at least one hour before serving. (Low Cholesterol)

Roba Ritt (Mrs. Clifford)

No Egg Cornflake Cookies

Yield: 3 dozen

2 c. flour
1 t. baking soda
1 c. margarine
¾ c. sugar
2 t. vanilla
cornflake crumbs

Combine all ingredients except crumbs, using pastry blender. Shape into walnut-size balls. Roll in cornflake crumbs. Flatten with fork. Bake at 350° for 20 minutes until golden brown. (Low Cholesterol)

Deborah-Ann Sappah

Almond Loaf Cake

Yield: 1 loaf

3 T. sweet butter (room temperature)
⅓ c. sugar
½ t. vanilla
¾ t. almond extract
1 egg yolk (room temperature)
⅔ c. (scant) flour
1 t. sodium-free baking powder
¼ c. milk (room temperature)

Mix together the first 5 ingredients; beat well. Mix together flour and baking powder; add to egg mixture alternately with milk. Beat well. Bake at between 325°-350° for 25 minutes in a 3½x6″ loaf pan. If desired frost with almond-flavored butter frosting. (Low Sodium)

Marian Stuart (Mrs. Russell)

Cinnamon Apple Cake

Serves 12-16

1 c. low cholesterol egg substitute
2 c. + 2 T sugar
1 c. polyunsaturated oil
4 tart apples, peeled, sliced
6 t. sugar
3 t. cinnamon
3 c. flour
3 t. baking powder
½ t. salt
½ c. orange juice
1 t. vanilla

Beat egg substitute until light yellow. Slowly add 1 cup sugar and oil and beat well. Combine flour, baking powder and salt. Combine orange juice and vanilla. Add flour and juice mixture alternately to the egg mixture, beating well after each addition. Combine remaining sugar and cinnamon. Pour ¼ of the batter into a greased and floured 10″ tube pan. Arrange ⅓ of apples on batter. Top with ⅓ of cinnamon mixture. Cover this with ⅓ more batter, then with remaining apples and cinnamon. Top with the remaining batter. Bake at 350° for one hour, 15 minutes; let cool 20 minutes; remove from pan. (Low Cholesterol coffee cake or dessert)

Roba Ritt (Mrs. Clifford)

Strawberry Devonshire Tart

Serves 8-10

Pastry shell:
1 c. flour
1 T. sugar
¼ c. + 2 T. margarine, softened
1 T. plus 1½ t. egg substitute
1 T. cold water

Filling:
1 3 oz. pkg. imitation cream cheese
3 T. low-fat sour cream
1-1½ qts. strawberries
¾ c. sugar
3 T. cornstarch
½ c. water
red food coloring (optional)

Mix flour, sugar and margarine with fork until crumbly. Add egg substitute and water; mix until dough holds together. Pat into flat round; wrap in plastic wrap; refrigerate until firm enough to roll. Place between two pieces of waxed paper. Wipe table with damp cloth to prevent paper from slipping. Roll pastry 2" larger than inverted 9" tart or pie pan. Peel off top paper; place in pan, paper side up. Peel off paper. Gently press in pan, trimming edges evenly. Refrigerate 1 hour. Bake at 375° for 15 minutes until light brown, pricking shell with fork when it begins to bubble.

Filling: Beat cream cheese until fluffy; beat in sour cream until smooth. Spread on bottom of baked shell; refrigerate. Mash enough berries to measure 1 cup. Force through sieve or use food processor; add enough water to measure 1 cup. Mix sugar and cornstarch; stir in water and the sieved berries. Cook, stirring constantly until thick. Boil, stirring, 1 minute. Remove from heat; cool slightly, stirring occasionally. Stir in food coloring. Arrange remaining whole berries, with tips up, in pastry shell. Pour cooked mixture on top. Refrigerate 1 hour. (Low Cholesterol — Low Sodium)

Joyce Margie (Mrs. Robert)

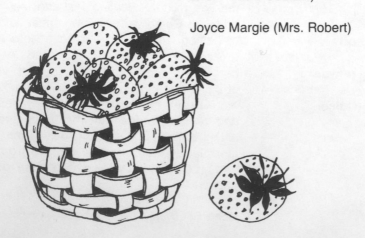

Low Fat Orange Mousse

Serves 6

6 oz. frozen orange
   juice
1 T. gelatin
2 T. cold water
2 T. orange liqueur
1 c. boiling water
1 c. low-fat creamed
   cottage cheese
¼ c. part-skim ricotta
   cheese
2 t. vanilla
grated orange peel
5 T. honey
orange sections

Thaw juice slightly. Sprinkle gelatin on water and liqueur in blender container. Add boiling water; blend at high speed, scraping often with rubber spatula until gelatin is dissolved. Add cheeses; blend until smooth. Add vanilla, orange peel, honey and partly thawed juice. Blend until juice is melted. Pour into a bowl; cover; chill 6-8 hours. Garnish with orange sections.

The Committee

Mixed Bag

Lemon Apples

6 Jonathan or Golden
  Delicious apples
1½ lemons, thinly sliced
1 c. water
½ c. sugar

Peel and quarter apples; cook with lemon slices in water until tender and clear, stirring in sugar for last few minutes. Drain well; set aside juice. Arrange apples on serving dish with lemons on top. Cool juice until jelly-like; pour over fruit. Serve chilled.

Florence Staplin (Mrs. William)

Cranberry Chutney

Yield: 2⅔ cups

2 c. cranberries, fresh
  or frozen
2 small tomatoes,
  peeled, seeded,
  coarsely chopped
¾ c. water
½ c. golden raisins
¼ c. chopped onion
1 t. salt
1 c. brown sugar,
  packed
½ c. cider vinegar
½ t. ground ginger
½ t. ground cloves
½ t. pepper

In a 3 quart saucepan combine cranberries, tomatoes, water, raisins, onion and salt. Bring to boiling. Simmer covered for 15 minutes until cranberries pop. Stir in remaining ingredients. Cover; cook 35-40 minutes until the consistency of relish, stirring occasionally. Ladle into jars or freezer containers. Refrigerate or freeze.

Helen Kelly (Mrs. Rowland)

Marmalade Grand Marnier

3 Temple oranges
2 medium lemons
½ grapefruit (peeled, if
  thick-skinned)
2 oz. Grand Marnier
sugar

Cut fruit in half; remove seeds. Slice thinly, discarding ends. Barely cover with cold water; add Grand Marnier. Cover and leave at room temperature overnight. Boil for 30 minutes. Cover and leave at room temperature overnight. Measure mixture; add equal amount of sugar (decrease by ½ cup if preferred tart). Cook slowly for 1 hour, stirring occasionally. Test by putting a few drops on a cold saucer; if runny, cook longer. Pour into sterilized glasses; seal.

Gloria O. Schrager, M.D.

Sauerkraut Relish

1   1 lb. can sauerkraut,
    drained
½ c. coarsely chopped
    onion
½ c. coarsely chopped
    green pepper
1   2 oz. jar pimiento,
    drained, chopped
1   c. sugar
1   c. cider vinegar

Mix sauerkraut, onion, green pepper and pimiento together. Boil together sugar and vinegar. When cooled, pour over sauerkraut mixture. Marinate at least 24 hours in refrigerator. Drain before serving. (This will keep up to two weeks if refrigerated in a glass container with tight-fitting lid.)

Jacqueline Poradek (Mrs. James)

Fire and Ice Tomatoes

6   large ripe firm
    tomatoes
1   large green pepper,
    sliced
1   red onion, sliced into
    rings
¾ c. vinegar
1½ t. celery salt
1½ t. mustard seed
½ t. salt
4½ t. sugar
⅛ t. red pepper
⅛ t. black pepper
¼ c. cold water
1   cucumber, peeled,
    sliced

Skin and quarter tomatoes. Combine with green pepper and onion. Set aside. Bring remaining ingredients except cucumber to a boil in saucepan; boil hard for 1 minute. While still hot pour over tomato mixture. Cool. Just before serving add cucumber. Serve as relish or side dish. Will keep for several days in refrigerator.

Chris Olson (Mrs. Charles)

Old-Fashioned Tomato Preserves

Yield: 12 6 oz. jars

5 lbs. firm ripe tomatoes
8 c. sugar
1 orange, thinly sliced
1 lemon, thinly sliced

Peel and quarter tomatoes. Cover with sugar; allow to stand overnight. Drain off syrup; heat syrup to boiling and cook until sugar spins a thread (232°). Add tomatoes and fruit slices. Cook over low heat until tomatoes are transparent. Seal in hot sterilized jars.

Gwen Moore (Mrs. David)

Pineapple Bake

Serves 4

¼ lb. butter, melted
5 slices bread, cubed
2 eggs
½ c. sugar
1 20 oz. can crushed
   pineapple
salt

Combine butter and bread; put into baking dish. Combine remaining ingredients; put on top of bread. Bake at 400° for 45-55 minutes. Before completely done, you may need to cover with foil to prevent burning. Good with ham.

Jane Rodimer (Mrs. Donald)

Baked Rabbit

Serves 2-4

1 rabbit, dressed and
   cut in pieces
melted butter
6 oz. dry white wine,
   divided
2 T. Dijon mustard
1 t. minced garlic
2 bay leaves
½ t. thyme
½ c. heavy cream

Baste rabbit liberally with butter; bake at 450° for 10 minutes, turning once and re-basting. Mix 2 teaspoons wine with mustard, brushing on all sides of rabbit; bake 5 minutes more. Add all other ingredients except cream. Cover tightly and bake at 375° for 45 minutes; baste occasionally. Add cream; bake 15 minutes more.

R. F. Wozniak, M.D.

Homemade Granola

Yield: 5-6 cups

4 c. rolled oats
½ c. sesame seeds
½ c. sunflower seeds
½ t. sea salt
¼ c. honey
¼ c. corn oil
1 t. vanilla
⅔ c. raisins
coconut, nuts, dates
(optional)

In large bowl combine oats, seeds and salt. Mix together honey, oil and vanilla; combine with oats mixture. Spread in shallow pan. Bake at 325° for 40 minutes until fairly dry and golden brown, stirring every 10 minutes. Remove from oven; add raisins.

Helen Hintz (Mrs. Edward)

Pecan Butter Crunch

1 c. butter
1⅓ c. sugar
¼ c. water
1 T. corn syrup
1 c. pecans, coarsely chopped
2 8 oz. bars milk chocolate
2 c. pecans, grated or finely chopped

Melt butter in large heavy saucepan. Add sugar, water and corn syrup, stirring frequently over medium heat to 300°. Toward end of cooking time, stir constantly. Add pecans. Pour evenly onto well greased 10x12" cookie sheet. Cool to room temperature. Melt 1 chocolate bar; spread on cooled candy. Sprinkle with half the grated pecans. Chill until chocolate is firm. Cover candy with waxed paper and invert quickly but carefully. Spread underside of candy with remaining chocolate, melted. Sprinkle with remaining pecans. Chill until chocolate is firm. Break into bite-sized pieces or cut into squares.

Claire Hadden (Mrs. William)

California Popped Corn

3 qts. freshly popped corn
⅓ c. butter, melted
2 T. (2 packets) G. Washington onion-flavored seasoning and broth mix
½ t. chili powder

Place popped corn in large baking pan. Combine remaining ingredients; cook 1 minute, stirring frequently. Pour over popped corn; toss lightly to mix. Bake at 300° for 10 minutes until hot and crisp. Store in a tightly covered contained up to 2 weeks.

Anne Jamison (Mrs. R. Barnett, Jr.)

Soft Pretzels

1 pkg. yeast
1½ c. warm water
⅛ t. ginger
1 T. sugar
1 t. salt
4 c. flour
1 egg, beaten
coarse salt

Dissolve yeast in warm water; stir in ginger. Add sugar and salt; blend in flour. Turn the dough out; knead on lightly floured board until smooth. Cut off 12-14 small pieces of dough; roll into ropes; twist into pretzel shape. Arrange on very lightly buttered cookie sheets. Brush with beaten egg; sprinkle with coarse salt. Bake at 425° for 15 minutes until browned.

Jacquelyn Marvin (Mrs. William)

Homemade Ice Cream Cones Yield: 8-10 cones

½ c. cake flour
¼ c. sugar
2 T. cornstarch
salt
¼ c. oil
2 egg whites
2 T. water
½ t. vanilla

Sift together dry ingredients. Add oil and egg whites; mix until smooth. Add water and vanilla. To make 1 cone at a time: pour about 1½ tablespoon batter onto hot, lightly greased griddle or skillet. Spread into 4″ circle. Cook over low heat 4 minutes until lightly browned. Turn; cook one minute. (Can use steak cuber to make patterned surface). Roll into wide mouthed cone shape. Secure with toothpick; cool on rack. Remove toothpicks.

Jacquelyn Marvin (Mrs. William)

Date Crispies

1 12 oz. pkg. chocolate
  chips
¼ c. shortening
½ c. butter
½ c. sugar
1½ c. chopped dates
1½ c. chopped pecans
1½ c. Rice Krispies
⅛ t. salt
½ t. vanilla

Melt half of chocolate and half of shortening in double boiler. Spread evenly into 8" square on waxed paper-lined cookie sheet; chill until firm. Melt remaining butter in large heavy pan. Stir in dates and nuts. Cook over medium heat, stirring constantly until butter is completely absorbed. Remove from heat; stir in Rice Krispies, salt and vanilla. Press mixture into a waxed paper-lined 8" square pan. Cool. Remove from pan by overturning onto chilled chocolate. Peel off waxed paper. Melt remaining chocolate and shortening; spread over date layer; chill. Return to room temperature before cutting into 64 pieces. Store in refrigerator.

Claire Hadden (Mrs. William)

Cocoa Mix

1 1 lb. box
  confectioners sugar
1 8 qt. pkg. instant
  powdered milk
1 6 oz. jar powdered
  cream (dairy
  substitute)
1 2 lb. box instant
  chocolate powder

Mix all ingredients together. For each cup of cocoa, fill mug ⅓ full with mix; add boiling water. (Good to keep on hand for children to make their own hot chocolate. It would also make a nice gift with a set of mugs.)

Jeanette Pease (Mrs. Franklin)

Fancy Chocolate Leaves

rose leaves
semi-sweet chocolate
   bits
watercolor paint brush

Leave a small stem on leaves for a handle; rinse; dry. Melt chocolate over hot water, stirring until smooth. With brush, paint underside of leaves with smooth, thick coating of chocolate, spreading just to edge. Refrigerate or freeze to set chocolate. To remove leaf from chocolate, insert tip of paring knife at tip of leaf; gently peel off. Refrigerate on waxed paper. Use as cake decoration, keeping chilled until serving time.

Jude Ferris (Mrs. A. Douglas)

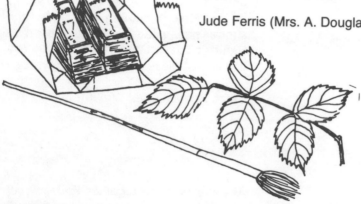

Chocolate Bird Nests

Yield: 18 nests

10-12   shredded wheat
   biscuits
1 12 oz. pkg. chocolate
   bits
4½ oz. chunky peanut
   butter
jelly beans

Finely crush biscuits. Melt chocolate in double boiler until just soft. Stir in peanut butter; add to shredded wheat. Drop by tablespoons onto waxed paper. Shape into nests. Place 3 jelly beans in each; chill.

Carole Witty (Mrs. Ronald)

Cappuccino

3 cinnamon sticks
12 cloves
½ c. instant expresso
   or ¾ c. instant
   decaffeinated coffee
6 c. boiling water
½ c. sugar
3 c. half and half cream,
   warmed
1 c. heavy cream,
   whipped
ground nutmeg

Tie cinnamon and cloves in cheesecloth; put in a saucepan. Add expresso and boiling water; steep for 5 minutes; remove spice bag. Stir in sugar and half and half. Serve in warmed cups; garnish with whipped cream and nutmeg.

Ann Low (Mrs. Calvin)

Viennese Iced Coffee

Serves 4

¼ c. powdered instant
   coffee
2 T. sugar
8 cloves
1 cinnamon stick
3 c. water
crushed ice
1 pt. vanilla ice-cream
½ c. heavy cream,
   whipped
ground cinnamon

Combine coffee, sugar, cloves, cinnamon stick and water; cover and bring to a boil. Remove from heat; let stand covered 5 minutes; strain and chill. Fill 4 chilled tall glasses ¼ full with crushed ice. Add a scoop of ice-cream to each; pour in coffee and muddle. Top each with cream and a dash of cinnamon.

Lois Oxenrider (Mrs. Bryce)

Champagne Punch

Yield: 4½ qts.

2 25 oz. bottles dry
   champagne
1 25 oz. bottle sauterne
1 6 oz. can frozen
   lemonade
1 pt. frozen lemon
   sherbert
1 46 oz. can pineapple
   juice
1-2 blocks ice, quart size
orange slices

Mix all ingredients except orange slices in a 6 quart bowl. Add ice blocks. Garnish with orange slices.

Lee Moore (Mrs. Robert)

Egg Nog

Yield: 2½ qts. 20 servings

12 eggs, separated
1 qt. heavy cream,
   whipped
1 pt. vanilla ice-cream,
   softened
confectioners sugar
vanilla
8 oz. white rum

Beat egg yolks; add to cream. Add stiffly
beaten egg whites. Gradually mix in ice-
cream. Add sugar, vanilla and rum. Serve
chilled.

Lee Moore (Mrs. Robert)

Frozen Strawberry Daiquiri

Yield: 24 oz.

1 12 oz. bottle 7-up
1 6 oz. can frozen
   lemonade
3 oz. frozen
   strawberries
3 oz. light rum

Blend all ingredients thoroughly in blender; freeze at least 4 hours.

For plain daiquiri, omit strawberries and
substitute 6 ounces frozen limeade for
lemonade.

Janie Bier (Mrs. Gregory)

Kahlua Liqueur

Yield: 3 fifth-size bottles

3 c. water
4 c. sugar
½ c. powdered instant
   coffee
¼ c. powdered instant
   expresso
1 fifth vodka, 100 proof
1 vanilla bean

Heat all ingredients, except vodka and
vanilla bean, until dissolved. Add vodka.
Divide equally into 3 bottles. Split vanilla
bean into thirds; place one-third in each
bottle. Seal; age for 3 weeks.

Josanne Swain (Mrs. James)

Pink Fluff

frozen pink lemonade
half and half cream
gin or vodka
crushed ice

Combine equal parts of lemonade,
cream, gin and ice in blender. Serve over
crushed ice.

Suzy Gumm (Mrs. Frederick)

Charlie's Red Wine Punch

Yield: 6 qts.

1 gal. burgundy
32 oz. frozen orange
   juice
1 qt. club soda
sugar
orange slices

Combine all ingredients except orange slices. Chill. Garnish with orange slices in punch bowl.

Ann Low (Mrs. Calvin)

Mulled Wine

Yield: 18 4 oz. servings

peel of 1 orange
peel of 1 lemon
2 cinnamon sticks
1 crushed whole
   nutmeg
10 cloves
½-¾ c. sugar
2-3 c. water
2 fifths burgundy,
   warmed

Combine all ingredients except burgundy. Simmer 10-15 minutes; strain. Add burgundy; heat just short of boiling. Serve warm.

Karen Rovick (Mrs. John)

Index

Entrees

Beef

Ground Beef

Lamb

Pork and Ham

Poultry

Chicken

Turkey

Seafood

Veal

Pasta

Pies and Pastries

Relishes and Accompaniments

Salads

COOKING IS OUR BAG
Overlook Hospital Auxiliary
Summit, New Jersey 07901

Send:

. . . . . copies of **COOKING IS OUR BAG** at $9.95
plus $1.35 postage and handling per book

☐   book gift wrapping and card at $.50

☐   co-ordinated 13x15″ canvas tote bag at $7.00
plus $1.35 postage and handling

☐   co-ordinated canvas butcher's apron at $7.00
plus $1.35 postage and handling

☐   **SPECIAL** — all 3 — at $21.95 plus $2.50 postage and handling

. . . . . total enclosed

Name ....

Address...

City .... State .... Zip ....

New Jersey residents add 5% sales tax

Make check payable to **Overlook Hospital Auxiliary Cookbook**

SEND GIFT BOOK TO:

Name ....

Address ....

City ....

State ....

Zip ....

COOKING IS OUR BAG
Overlook Hospital Auxiliary
Summit, New Jersey 07901

Send:

. . . . . copies of **COOKING IS OUR BAG** at $9.95
plus $1.35 postage and handling per book

☐   book gift wrapping and card at $.50

☐   co-ordinated 13x15″ canvas tote bag at $7.00
plus $1.35 postage and handling

☐   co-ordinated canvas butcher's apron at $7.00
plus $1.35 postage and handling

☐   **SPECIAL** — all 3 — at $21.95 plus $2.50 postage and handling

. . . . . total enclosed

Name ....

Address...

City .... State .... Zip ....

New Jersey residents add 5% sales tax

Make check payable to **Overlook Hospital Auxiliary Cookbook**

SEND GIFT BOOK TO:

Name ....

Address ....

City ....

State ....

Zip ....

COOKING IS OUR BAG
Overlook Hospital Auxiliary
Summit, New Jersey 07901

Send:

. . . . . copies of **COOKING IS OUR BAG** at $9.95
                plus $1.35 postage and handling per book

☐   book gift wrapping and card at $.50

☐   co-ordinated 13x15" canvas tote bag at $7.00
                plus $1.35 postage and handling

☐   co-ordinated canvas butcher's apron at $7.00
                plus $1.35 postage and handling

☐   **SPECIAL** — all 3 — at $21.95 plus $2.50 postage and handling

. . . . . total enclosed

Name ....
Address..
City .... State .... Zip ....

New Jersey residents add 5% sales tax

Make check payable to **Overlook Hospital Auxiliary Cookbook**

SEND GIFT BOOK TO:

Name ....
Address ....
City ....
State ....
Zip ....

COOKING IS OUR BAG
Overlook Hospital Auxiliary
Summit, New Jersey 07901

Send:

. . . . . copies of **COOKING IS OUR BAG** at $9.95
                plus $1.35 postage and handling per book

☐   book gift wrapping and card at $.50

☐   co-ordinated 13x15" canvas tote bag at $7.00
                plus $1.35 postage and handling

☐   co-ordinated canvas butcher's apron at $7.00
                plus $1.35 postage and handling

☐   **SPECIAL** — all 3 — at $21.95 plus $2.50 postage and handling

. . . . . total enclosed

Name ....
Address..
City .... State .... Zip ....

New Jersey residents add 5% sales tax

Make check payable to **Overlook Hospital Auxiliary Cookbook**

SEND GIFT BOOK TO:

Name ....
Address ....
City ....
State ....
Zip ....